The Kingdom in History and Prophecy

Lewis Sperry Chafer

SOJOURNER
PRESS

Editing by Peter Goeman

Cover design by Sojourner Press

ISBN 978-1-960255-00-6 (Paperback)

ISBN 978-1-960255-01-3 (Epub)

Printed in the United States of America
Sojourner Press
Raleigh, NC
sojournerpress.org

For bulk, special sales, or ministry purchases, please contact us at sales@sojournerpress.org.

Dedicated to the memory of my father
The Rev. Thomas Franklin Chafer
with the Lord since 1882

Contents

Introduction

A clear and thoroughly Biblical book on the kingdom in the Scriptures has long been a *desideratum*. Perhaps no truth of the divine revelation has suffered more at the hands of interpreters than that concerning the kingdom. Following the Roman Catholic interpretation, Protestant theology has very generally taught that all the kingdom promises, and even the great Davidic Covenant itself, are to be fulfilled in and through the Church. The confusion thus created has been still further darkened by the failure to distinguish the different phases of kingdom truth indicated by the expressions "kingdom of heaven," and "kingdom of God."

In the light of plain Scripture all of these confusions are inexcusable, for at no point is the Biblical revelation more clear and explicit. Founded upon the covenant of Jehovah with David, a covenant subsequently confirmed by Jehovah's oath, the great theme of predictive prophecy is that kingdom. Even the order of the setting up of the kingdom, relatively to the great Gentile world empires, is declared. The events attending the setting up of the kingdom of the heavens on the earth are described.

The New Testament carries forward the Old Testament foreview of the kingdom into greater detail, but without change. The very first mention of Christ in the first verse of the first chapter in the New Testament identifies Him with the Davidic Covenant, and the promise of Gabriel to His virgin mother is a new confirmation in express terms of that covenant.

The New Testament reveals the present age as a parenthesis in the prophetic program during which the Church is called out from among the Gentiles, a stranger and pilgrim body, belonging to the kingdom of God, but in no sense identical with the kingdom of heaven.

I welcome therefore this present book on these fundamental truths. Having had the privilege of seeing it in manuscript, I bespeak for it the candid attention of all who are concerned for the truth of God.

C. I. Scofield
"Greyshingles," Douglaston, NY

Introduction to the Revised Edition

Lewis Sperry Chafer (1871–1952) was a renowned American theologian who wrote prolifically on systematic theology. He is perhaps most well known as the co-founder and first president of Dallas Theological Seminary. He was an early advocate of dispensationalism and was the teacher of Charles Ryrie, who became one of the champions of the movement.

Chafer's *The Kingdom in History and Prophecy* is now over 100 years old, but it remains an excellent example of biblical exegesis which is driven by an originalist hermeneutic and not a theological system. As such, it is a work that students of Scripture should be familiar with if they are interested in understanding the theme of the kingdom.

The most significant change from the 1915 edition is that the Scripture citations and quotes from Chafer have been updated from the KJV to the ESV. I also updated the biblical texts to include the chapter and verse references where appropriate. Antiquated vocabulary and grammar have also been updated. As such, this revised edition provides the modern reader with a valuable resource on the King and His kingdom.

Peter Goeman, 2023
Raleigh, NC

Preface

Many valuable books have been written on the general subjects related to the kingdom. A partial list of these is appended herewith; but no similar work covering, in brief form, the historic and prophetic aspects of the kingdom in their relation to the present age-purpose was known to the writer: hence this volume. It is hoped that this book will prove a comprehensive, if not exhaustive, treatise on this important theme.

It has not seemed expedient to deal with all problems of interpretation when they first appear in the discussion. Therefore the general difficulties arising in this study are taken up, so far as the writer is able, in what may seem to him to be the most appropriate place, and the reader to whom this interpretation is new is requested to withhold all judgments and conclusions until the various aspects of this revelation, here dealt with, have been considered.

May the Spirit, whose office work it is to guide into all truth and to show us things to come, guide the study of what it has pleased our God to reveal of His purpose and plan in the realization of His kingdom in the earth.

Lewis Sperry Chafer
Upper Montclair, NJ

1

The Theme

The Bible revelation regarding the kingdom presents the purpose, process, and final realization of a divine government in the earth. This objective is the heart of the kingdom prayer: "Your kingdom come, your will be done, *on earth* as it is in heaven." The kingdom revelation is a distinct body of Scripture running through both the Old Testament and the New and its study, of necessity, leads to some definite conclusions touching the meaning of much unfulfilled prophecy, two advents of Christ, the present age of Grace and the future of both Jews and Gentiles.

Considering only kingdom passages, both historical and prophetic, such definite conclusions are not difficult from the fact that this revelation is presented in those Scriptures which are more easily harmonized than the familiar body of truth from which are drawn the doctrines of salvation. Salvation revelations are sufficiently clear; but upon them the theological discussions of centuries have been centered. On the other hand, such general study has not been given to kingdom truths. In fact, many students of theology are confessedly ignorant on this subject. However, there is no conflict between Salvation and Kingdom themes. They cover widely different fields of Biblical doctrine.

In view of these facts, it may be helpful to note some of the essential values accruing from, and conditions governing, the study of kingdom truth.

Bible interpretation is incomplete without it.

It stands to reason, since one-fourth of the Bible is in prophetic form, and five-sixths of the Bible is addressed to one nation to whom the kingdom promises are given, that any plan of study which avoids prophecy and ignores, or "spiritualizes," God's covenants with His chosen earthly people will be incomplete, misleading and subject to mere human assumptions.

The accurate study of the kingdom in the Old Testament and the New affords the only comprehensible approach to the New Testament doctrines of "the present evil age" (Gal 1:4), "the church which is his body" (Eph 1:22–23), and "things to come" (John 16:13).

It has been pointed out that two distinct revelations were given to the Apostle Paul. In Arabia he received directly from God the gospel of grace (Gal 1:11–12) which he has presented, in the main, in the Roman and Galatian letters. This is a revelation of a new order, a new relationship to God, which is neither a perpetuation of Judaism, nor a modification of that system. Judaism remains intact and follows its predicted course, according to Scripture, to the end. The new revelation of the grace of God which has appeared, and which is made possible only by the cross, should not be colored by the Judaic teaching. It is a complete system in itself and, like Judaism, continues intact to its predicted end. For what else is Paul contending in Galatians if it is not that these two distinct systems shall not be mixed? And yet to what seeming avail are those pleadings to law-ridden, Judaized Protestantism today?

The second revelation came, in the main, from Paul's two years of imprisonment. This body of truth embraces the plan of the ages, the whole doctrine of the Church and the present out-calling of a heavenly body and bride as recorded in the Ephesian and Colossian letters. It is this advance body of truth which is never comprehended apart from the exact lines of distinctions laid down in kingdom revelations.

Theology, as usually presented, is disproportionately concerned with the Arabian revelation and a grave harm is done when such theology, creeds or catechisms, built largely on one aspect of New Testament teaching, are supposed to be adequate interpretations of the whole divine revelation. The theological student who enters his ministry with such presuppositions and limitations, inaccurate in many of his conceptions and prejudiced toward whole bodies of truth about which he knows little, will be incompetent to minister the whole Word.

An illustration of this may be drawn from 1 Timothy 4:1–6. It is set forth here that the young Timothy may win the high title of "a good servant of Christ Jesus," if he is faithful in putting the brethren in remembrance of the awful apostasy with which the present age must end (see also 2 Thess 2:1–10). How shall any minister discern an age-closing apostasy with its divinely ordered relations to the final triumph of God in the earth if he does not know these exact revelations which form the whole program of the kingdom according to Scripture?

No minister, therefore, can "preach the Word" in its right proportions, or be a "good servant of Christ Jesus" who habitually ignores the great prophetic themes. Nor is he excused in his neglect, or prejudice, by virtue of the fact that he represents a majority, or that other ideals have been set before him by his teachers. What is the particular knowledge that gives proficiency to the minister of Christ if it is not a thorough understanding of the Scriptures? Successful men of other professions apply themselves continually to the acquirement of accurate knowledge covering every phase of their chosen calling. Are these the accepted standards of the ministerial profession? Would we choose to be operated on by a physician who knows no more of surgery than the average theological student knows about prophecy? Yet the knowledge of prophecy in its main features, is distinctly a part, and a very large and qualifying part, of the material committed to those who are called to "preach the Word."

Knowledge of prophetic truth qualifies all intelligent Christian life and service.

The careful student who distinguishes the various purposes of God in the ages, has discovered that there is a distinct rule of life and program for service in the present age which can never, reasonably, be confused with that which has gone before, or that which is to follow. It is a serious mistake to press law-observance in the face of repeated revelations that the believer of this age is not under law as his rule of life (Rom 6:14; 10:4, 5; Gal 5:18; 2 Cor 3:11, 17). So also it will be found that, at present, service is the accomplishment of divine undertakings never before revealed and its motives are alone the mighty governing principles of grace. A real zeal in service will result and a beginning of interest in Bible study will develop when these plain distinctions are carefully taught and observed.

Kingdom and prophetic truths are being falsely represented.

The country is being swept by "Russellism" (so-called "Millennial Dawn," "International Bible Students' League," etc.), and the appalling progress of this system which so misrepresents the whole revelation of God can only be accounted for in the unsatisfied hunger of the people for the prophetic portions of Scripture. Such a false system, mixing truth with untruth, and designed to interpret all of the divine revelation, is evidently more engaging to the popular mind than only the Scriptural presentation of the fundamental doctrines concerning God, Man and Redemption. Satan's lies are always garnished with truth and how much more attractive they seem to be when that garnishing is a neglected truth! And insurance against the encroachment of such false teaching lies only in correctly presenting the whole body of truth rather than in treating any portion of it as impractical or dangerous. No minister need greatly fear any false system when he is intelligently and constantly feeding the people on the Word in all its symmetry and due proportions. This is not only true concerning the teachings of "Millennial Dawn," but is equally true of the teachings of "Christian Science," "New Thought," "Spiritism," "Seventh Day Adventism" and all unscriptural doctrines of Sanctification.

Unfulfilled prophecy is as credible as history.

No one will question that faith is taxed in the study of prophecy more than in the study of history. It is not difficult to believe what has assuredly taken place: it is quite another thing to believe confidently that unprecedented events will occur when based only on the bare predictions of Scripture. This failure in faith doubtless underlies much neglect of the prophetic Scriptures and accounts for a prevalent habit of allegorizing and qualifying prophecy until it is reduced to the limitation of a human opinion. Under this pressure men otherwise clear on the interpretation of the Bible have gone so far as to assert that what Paul wrote in his early ministry was abandoned or qualified in his later ministry. Revelation requires no such surgery. Such efforts reveal a state of mind which finds it easier to diminish Biblical authority than to increase personal confidence in the accuracy of Scripture. The mighty revelations of the purpose of God cannot be apprehended until the issue of believing his Word has been faithfully met.

Prophetic language is equally as accurate as other Scriptures.

While some prophecy is couched in symbolic language, those portions which trace the forward movements of the kingdom in the earth are largely free from problems presented by such symbolism, and that body of truth appears in language and terms the meaning of which cannot reasonably be questioned. The pity is that Origen ever conceived the allegorizing method of interpretation, and that his misleading and violent liberty with the text has since found such fertile soil in which to propagate.

A mixture of the teachings concerning Israel, as a nation, with the revelations concerning the Church, the body of Christ, is groundless in Scripture. It is hopelessly confusing and grotesque, for under this plan only Israel's blessings are borrowed; her curses and penalties are, naturally, not wanted. No progress can be made in the kingdom studies unless plain words are taken in their obviously plain meaning. In the Bible "Israel" is not the "Church;" "Zion" is not the body of saints of this dispensation; the "throne of David" is not heaven, nor will it ever be; the "land of your fathers" is not "Paradise" and the "house of Jacob" is not a host of Gentiles ignorantly attempting to force an entrance into Judaism. All such borrowed habits of interpretation must be faithfully judged and abandoned if ever the kingdom portions of God's Word are to assume any order or meaning.

Scripture must be rightly divided and applied.

It has been said "All Scripture is for us, but all Scripture is not about us." It all bears a message to us, but is not all our rule of life. It will not do for Gentile believers to read themselves into the great portion of the Bible which treats distinctly of a chosen nation, still a separate people in the earth, under the special unbroken purpose of God and exactly where God intended them to be at this very hour.

So with Christ: He was "a servant to the circumcised to show God's truthfulness, in order to confirm the promises given to the patriarchs" (Rom 15:8). This describes a strictly Jewish mission and purpose. He was also the grounds of personal justification to the Gentile believers (1 Cor 1:3–8; 2 Cor 5:21); but the two are separate. Because He was great enough to fulfill the predicted requirements for both Jew and Gentile is no warrant for Gentiles to attempt to intrude into those divine ministrations which were evidently only for the Jews. A right division and application of Scripture demands that a portion of the earthly life and ministry of Jesus be recognized as belonging to the divine covenants with one nation in which Gentiles have no part (Eph 2:11–12). During these ministrations Gentiles were not in view (Matt 10:5) nor can they be made to so appear by any fair method of interpretation.

There can be but one true system of interpretation.

It is for the faithful student to discover this for himself. Accepted inferences of so-called Postmillennialism and Premillennialism as possible co-existing systems of interpretation constitute a serious challenge against the dignity and purpose of the Bible itself. Either the divine revelation follows a definite order in the development of the kingdom in the earth, or it does not. If it does, there could hardly be two distinct programs coexisting in the mind and purpose of God. If there is but one order, an individual who confessedly knows nothing of the kingdom body of truth falls far short of being an approved workman, rightly dividing the Word of Truth, when he, through prejudice or preconceived conclusions, is not willing to be moved and molded by the exact and accurate words of revelation. And how much greater is his failure when guilty of withholding these mighty transforming themes from others!

2

The Kingdom Covenanted

The Bible teaches that God will ultimately triumph over all sin and rebellion in the earth. This is stated in many passages; notably 1 Corinthians 15:24–28:

> "Then comes the end, when he delivers the kingdom to
> God the Father after destroying every rule and every au-
> thority and power. For he must reign until he has put all
> his enemies under his feet. The last enemy to be destroyed
> is death. For 'God has put all things in subjection under
> his feet.' But when it says, 'all things are put in subjection,'
> it is plain that he is excepted who put all things in sub-
> jection under him. When all things are subjected to him,
> then the Son himself will also be subjected to him who
> put all things in subjection under him, that God may be
> all in all."

Thus does the divine record predict the restoration of this universe to its primal blessedness under the unchallenged authority of God, when the Son shall have put down all authority and banished every foe. This purpose, as recorded in the Bible, appears in various stages, or aspects, all leading with the certainty of the Infinite to the glorious consummation.

The reestablishment of the authority of God is first mentioned in Genesis 3:15, where it is stated that the Seed of the woman should bruise the head of Satan, the file leader of all the permitted present confusion in the government of God. In this mighty undertaking, too, Satan must bruise his heel. There are successive methods and various degrees of divine government in the earth following this first reference in Genesis and leading up to the eternal kingdom covenant made with David. In the Davidic Covenant the final consummation is again foreseen in that this covenant is unlimited in respect to time. It is the detail and duration of this covenant that gives it preeminent value as the logical starting point for all kingdom study in the Scriptures. The portion of the Davidic Covenant which has to do with eternal rule and government is as follows:

> "Moreover, the LORD declares to you that the LORD will make you a house. When your days are fulfilled and you lie down with your fathers, I will raise up your offspring after you, who shall come from your body, and I will establish his kingdom. He shall build a house for my name, and I will establish the throne of his kingdom forever. I will be to him a father, and he shall be to me a son. When he commits iniquity, I will discipline him with the rod of men, with the stripes of the sons of men, but my steadfast love will not depart from him, as I took it from Saul, whom I put away from before you. And your house and your kingdom shall be made sure forever before me. Your throne shall be established forever" (2 Sam 7:11–16).

This covenant, as herein stated, secures an established kingly order which will continue forever. The element of perpetuity in this kingly rule was not conditioned in Jehovah's oath by sin in the Davidic house. Chastisement was provided in case of disobedience—chastisement which fell upon the nation in the captivities and the dispersion—but the eternal purpose of the covenant is not abrogated: "Your throne shall be established forever." Of this eternal covenant and the one condition of chastisement it is written in Psalm 89:20–37:

"I have found David, my servant; with my holy oil I have anointed him, so that my hand shall be established with him; my arm also shall strengthen him. The enemy shall not outwit him; the wicked shall not humble him. I will crush his foes before him and strike down those who hate him. My faithfulness and my steadfast love shall be with him, and in my name shall his horn be exalted. I will set his hand on the sea and his right hand on the rivers. He shall cry to me, 'You are my Father, my God, and the Rock of my salvation.' And I will make him the firstborn, the highest of the kings of the earth. My steadfast love I will keep for him forever, and my covenant will stand firm for him. I will establish his offspring forever and his throne as the days of the heavens. If his children forsake my law and do not walk according to my rules, if they violate my statutes and do not keep my commandments, then I will punish their transgression with the rod and their iniquity with stripes, but I will not remove from him my steadfast love or be false to my faithfulness. I will not violate my covenant or alter the word that went forth from my lips. Once for all I have sworn by my holiness; I will not lie to David. His offspring shall endure forever, his throne as long as the sun before me. Like the moon it shall be established forever, a faithful witness in the skies."

The certainty of this covenant is again stated in Jeremiah 33:20–21:

"Thus says the LORD: If you can break my covenant with the day and my covenant with the night, so that day and night will not come at their appointed time, then also my covenant with David my servant may be broken, so that he shall not have a son to reign on his throne...."

Peter, by the Spirit, in his pentecostal sermon reveals also that it was the eternal element in this covenant, to which Jehovah had sworn with an oath, that led David to foresee the Lord always before his face and to demand in his faith, even the resurrection of Christ, that the oath of his God should not fail. Thus Peter spoke of David:

> "For David says concerning him, 'I saw the Lord always before me, for he is at my right hand that I may not be shaken; therefore my heart was glad, and my tongue rejoiced; my flesh also will dwell in hope. For you will not abandon my soul to Hades, or let your Holy One see corruption. You have made known to me the paths of life; you will make me full of gladness with your presence.' Brothers, I may say to you with confidence about the patriarch David that he both died and was buried, and his tomb is with us to this day. Being therefore a prophet, and knowing that God had sworn with an oath to him that he would set one of his descendants on his throne, he foresaw and spoke about the resurrection of the Christ, that he was not abandoned to Hades, nor did his flesh see corruption" (Acts 2:25–31).

So, yet again, when the reign of peace through David's Greater Son is pictured to the House of Jacob, over whom he is to rule, the same eternal covenant is mentioned with a chastisement: "In overflowing anger for a moment I hid my face from you," which moment, however, has already extended at least twenty-four centuries; but what is this compared with that which follows: "But with everlasting love I will have compassion on you, says the LORD, your Redeemer" (Isa 54:8).

The history of the kings from David on, with the sin of the nation, is too familiar to need description. Their complete apostasy ended in chastisement in which they were taken off from the land and scattered among the nations and there was a cessation of the line of kings. These exact events Moses had prophesied a full thousand years before. This prophecy forms a part of the farewell address of Moses to the nation for whom he had wrought, and with whom, because of the judgments of Jehovah, he could not enter the land. Moses foresaw the national apostasy, the chastisement by exile, and on beyond a period already extended 3,500 years, to that nation's blessings which are yet future, when their chastisement shall have ended and they are regathered into their own land under the unchanging covenant of Jehovah. These prophecies are recorded in Deuteronomy 26:1 to 30:20. Only a portion is here given:

> "And as the LORD took delight in doing you good and multiplying you, so the LORD will take delight in bringing ruin upon you and destroying you. And you shall be plucked off the land that you are entering to take possession of it. And the LORD will scatter you among all peoples, from one end of the earth to the other, and there you shall serve other gods of wood and stone, which neither you nor your fathers have known. And among these nations you shall find no respite, and there shall be no resting place for the sole of your foot, but the LORD will give you there a trembling heart and failing eyes and a languishing soul. Your life shall hang in doubt before you. Night and day you shall be in dread and have no assurance of your life. In the morning you shall say, 'If only it were evening!' and at evening you shall say, 'If only it were morning!' because of the dread that your heart shall feel, and the sights that your eyes shall see. And the LORD will bring you back in ships to Egypt, a journey that I promised that you should never make again; and there you shall offer yourselves for sale to your enemies as male and female slaves, but there will be no buyer" (Deut 28:63–68).

> "And when all these things come upon you, the blessing and the curse, which I have set before you, and you call

them to mind among all the nations where the LORD
your God has driven you, and return to the LORD your
God, you and your children, and obey his voice in all that
I command you today, with all your heart and with all
your soul, then the LORD your God will restore your
fortunes and have mercy on you, and he will gather you
again from all the peoples where the LORD your God has
scattered you. If your outcasts are in the uttermost parts
of heaven, from there the LORD your God will gather
you, and from there he will take you. And the LORD
your God will bring you into the land that your fathers
possessed, that you may possess it. And he will make you
more prosperous and numerous than your fathers. And
the LORD your God will circumcise your heart and the
heart of your offspring, so that you will love the LORD
your God with all your heart and with all your soul, that
you may live. And the LORD your God will put all these
curses on your foes and enemies who persecuted you. And
you shall again obey the voice of the LORD and keep
all his commandments that I command you today. The
LORD your God will make you abundantly prosperous
in all the work of your hand, in the fruit of your womb and
in the fruit of your cattle and in the fruit of your ground.
For the LORD will again take delight in prospering you,
as he took delight in your fathers, when you obey the voice
of the LORD your God, to keep his commandments and
his statutes that are written in this Book of the Law, when
you turn to the LORD your God with all your heart and
with all your soul" (Deut 30:1–10).

There is no more important Scripture relating to Israel than this, and
every word of this prophecy covering the time to the present hour has
been literally fulfilled. Shall it not be so to the end? Shall they not be
regathered as actually as they have been scattered? And that in relation

to, and by virtue of, a "return," or second coming (30:3) of the divine Person to the earth? Is there any other explanation of the miraculous preservation of that nation than that Jehovah's oath cannot be broken?

3

The Kingdom Prophesied

It is significant that the Old Testament prophets spoke, in the main, in one comparatively brief period. This was the time in which Israel was approaching and entering her national dispersion under the chastening hand of God. It was in the darkest hour of their history that these seers, as by contrast, set forth the unprecedented light of the nation's coming glory. This consensus of prophetic vision has never had a semblance of fulfillment; yet the nation is still divinely preserved, and that, evidently, with this consummation in view (Jer 31:35–37; Matt 24:31–34).

Some of the prophets spoke before the exile, some during the exile, while others spoke after a remnant, but not the nation, had returned to their land. While they spoke with individual purpose and style, they were united as one voice on certain great themes. They condemned the nation's sin and predicted the coming chastisement. They saw the judgments about to fall upon the surrounding nations; but these Gentile judgments are in view only as they are related to Israel. Above all they saw their own future blessings, the form and manner of which are too accurately described by them to be misunderstood. Their prophecies expanded into magnificent detail the covenanted reign of David's Son over the House of Jacob forever.

In tracing these passages scarcely a comment is necessary if the statements are taken in their plain and obvious meaning. Passages are here selected from the many that were spoken by all the prophets concerning the coming King and His kingdom, and from these Scriptures the following will be seen.

Immanuel's kingdom will be theocratic.

The King will be (a) "Immanuel, God with us;" (b) by human birth a rightful heir to David's throne; (c) born of a virgin in Bethlehem.

(*a*) The King will be "Immanuel, God with us."

- "Therefore the Lord himself will give you a sign. Behold, the virgin shall conceive and bear a son, and shall call his name Immanuel" (Isa 7:14).

- "All this took place to fulfill what the Lord had spoken by the prophet: 'Behold, the virgin shall conceive and bear a son, and they shall call his name Immanuel' (which means, God with us)" (Matt 1:22–23).

(*b*) The King will be heir to David's throne.

- "There shall come forth a shoot from the stump of Jesse, and a branch from his roots shall bear fruit. And the Spirit of the Lord shall rest upon him, the Spirit of wisdom and understanding, the Spirit of counsel and might, the Spirit of knowledge and the fear of the Lord. And his delight shall be in the fear of the Lord. He shall not judge by what his eyes see, or decide disputes by what his ears hear, but with righteousness he shall judge the poor, and decide with equity for the meek of the earth; and he shall strike the earth with the rod of his mouth, and with the breath of his lips he shall kill the wicked. Righteousness shall be the belt of his waist, and faithfulness the belt of his loins" (Isa 11:1–5).

- "Behold, the days are coming, declares the LORD, when I will raise up for David a righteous Branch, and he shall reign as king and deal wisely, and shall execute justice and righteousness in the land" (Jer 23:5).

- "And I will set up over them one shepherd, my servant David, and he shall feed them: he shall feed them and be their shepherd" (Ezek 34:23).

- "My servant David shall be king over them, and they shall all have one shepherd. They shall walk in my rules and be careful to obey my statutes" (Ezek 37:24).

- "For the children of Israel shall dwell many days without king or prince, without sacrifice or pillar, without ephod or household gods. Afterward the children of Israel shall return and seek the LORD their God, and David their king, and they shall come in fear to the LORD and to his goodness in the latter days" (Hos 3:4–5).

(c) The King was to be born of a virgin in Bethlehem.

- "Therefore the Lord himself will give you a sign. Behold, the virgin shall conceive and bear a son, and shall call his name Immanuel" (Isa 7:14).

- "But you, O Bethlehem Ephrathah, who are too little to be among the clans of Judah, from you shall come forth for me one who is to be ruler in Israel, whose coming forth is from of old, from ancient days" (Mic 5:2).

Immanuel's kingdom will be heavenly in character.

- "He shall judge between the nations, and shall decide disputes for many peoples; and they shall beat their swords into plowshares, and their spears into pruning hooks; nation shall not lift up sword against nation, neither shall they learn war anymore" (Isa 2:4).

- "But with righteousness he shall judge the poor, and decide with equity for the meek of the earth; and he shall strike the earth with the rod of his mouth, and with the breath of his lips he shall kill the wicked. Righteousness shall be the belt of his waist, and faithfulness the belt of his loins" (Isa 11:4–5).

- "Behold, the days are coming, declares the LORD, when I will fulfill the promise I made to the house of Israel and the house of Judah. In those days and at that time I will cause a righteous Branch to spring up for David, and he shall execute justice and righteousness in the land. In those days Judah will be saved, and Jerusalem will dwell securely. And this is the name by which it will be called: 'The LORD is our righteousness.' For thus says the LORD: David shall never lack a man to sit on the throne of the house of Israel" (Jer 33:14–17).

- "And I will make for them a covenant on that day with the beasts of the field, the birds of the heavens, and the creeping things of the ground. And I will abolish the bow, the sword, and war from the land, and I will make you lie down in safety" (Hos 2:18).

Immanuel's kingdom will be (a) in the earth; (b) centered at Jerusalem; (c) over regathered and converted Israel; (d) and extending to the nations.

(a) Immanuel's kingdom will be in the earth.

- "Ask of me, and I will make the nations your heritage, and the ends of the *earth* your possession" (Ps 2:8).

- "They shall not hurt or destroy in all my holy mountain; for the *earth* shall be full of the knowledge of the LORD as the waters cover the sea" (Isa 11:9).

- "He will not grow faint or be discouraged till he has established justice in the *earth*; and the coastlands wait for his law" (Isa 42:4).

- "Behold, the days are coming, declares the LORD, when I will raise up for David a righteous Branch, and he shall reign as king and deal wisely, and shall execute justice and righteousness in the *land*" (Jer 23:5).

- "And the LORD will be king over all the *earth*. On that day the LORD will be one and his name one" (Zech 14:9).

(b) Immanuel's kingdom will be centered at Jerusalem.

- "The word that Isaiah the son of Amoz saw concerning Judah and Jerusalem. It shall come to pass in the latter days that the mountain of the house of the LORD shall be established as the highest of the mountains, and shall be lifted up above the hills; and all the nations shall flow to it, and many peoples shall come, and say: 'Come, let us go up to the mountain of the LORD, to the house of the God of Jacob, that he may teach us his ways and that we may walk in his paths.' For out of Zion shall go forth the law, and the word of the LORD from Jerusalem" (Isa 2:1–3).

- "For Zion's sake I will not keep silent, and for Jerusalem's sake I will not be quiet, until her righteousness goes forth as brightness, and her salvation as a burning torch. The nations shall see your righteousness, and all the kings your glory, and you shall be called by a new name that the mouth of the LORD will give. You shall be a crown of beauty in the hand of the LORD, and a royal diadem in the hand of your God. You shall no more be termed Forsaken, and your land shall no more be termed Desolate, but you shall be called My Delight Is in Her, and your land Married; for the LORD delights in you, and your land shall be married. For as a young man marries a young woman, so shall your sons marry you, and as the bridegroom rejoices over the bride, so shall your God rejoice over you. On your walls, O Jerusalem, I have set watchmen; all the day and all the night they shall never be silent. You who put the LORD in remembrance, take no rest, and give him no rest until he establishes Jerusalem and makes it a praise in the earth" (Isa 62:1–7).

- "Thus says the LORD of hosts: Peoples shall yet come, even the inhabitants of many cities. The inhabitants of one city shall go to another, saying, 'Let us go at once to entreat the favor of the LORD and to seek the LORD of hosts; I myself am going.' Many peoples and strong nations shall come to seek the LORD of hosts in Jerusalem and to entreat the favor of the LORD. Thus says the LORD of hosts: In those days ten men from the nations of every tongue shall take hold of the robe of a Jew, saying, 'Let us go with you, for we have heard that God is with you'" (Zech 8:20–23).

- "And Jerusalem will be trampled underfoot by the Gentiles, until the times of the Gentiles are fulfilled" (Luke 21:24).

(c) Immanuel's kingdom will be over regathered and converted Israel.

- "Then the LORD your God will restore your fortunes and have mercy on you, and he will gather you again from all the peoples where the LORD your God has scattered you. If your outcasts are in the uttermost parts of heaven, from there the LORD your God will gather you, and from there he will take you. And the LORD your God will bring you into the land that your fathers possessed, that you may possess it. And he will make you more prosperous and numerous than your fathers. And the

LORD your God will circumcise your heart and the heart of your offspring, so that you will love the LORD your God with all your heart and with all your soul, that you may live" (Deut 30:3–6).

- "In that day the Lord will extend his hand yet a second time to recover the remnant that remains of his people, from Assyria, from Egypt, from Pathros, from Cush, from Elam, from Shinar, from Hamath, and from the coastlands of the sea. He will raise a signal for the nations and will assemble the banished of Israel, and gather the dispersed of Judah from the four corners of the earth" (Isa 11:11–12).

- "For the LORD will have compassion on Jacob and will again choose Israel, and will set them in their own land, and sojourners will join them and will attach themselves to the house of Jacob. And the peoples will take them and bring them to their place, and the house of Israel will possess them in the LORD's land as male and female slaves. They will take captive those who were their captors, and rule over those who oppressed them" (Isa 14:1–2; see also Isa 60:1–22).

- "In his days Judah will be saved, and Israel will dwell securely. And this is the name by which he will be called: 'The LORD is our righteousness.' Therefore, behold, the days are coming, declares the LORD, when they shall no longer say, 'As the LORD lives who brought up the people of Israel out of the land of Egypt,' but 'As the LORD lives who brought up and led the offspring of the house of Israel out of the north country and out of all the countries where he had driven them.' Then they shall dwell in their own land" (Jer 23:6–8).

- "Behold, I will gather them from all the countries to which I drove them in my anger and my wrath and in great indignation. I will bring them back to this place, and I will make them dwell in safety. And they shall be my people, and I will be their God"

(Jer 32:37–38).

- "I will restore the fortunes of Judah and the fortunes of Israel, and rebuild them as they were at first. I will cleanse them from all the guilt of their sin against me, and I will forgive all the guilt of their sin and rebellion against me. And this city shall be to me a name of joy, a praise and a glory before all the nations of the earth who shall hear of all the good that I do for them. They shall fear and tremble because of all the good and all the prosperity I provide for it" (Jer 33:7–9; see also Ezek 36:16–38).

- "Then say to them, Thus says the Lord GOD: Behold, I will take the people of Israel from the nations among which they have gone, and will gather them from all around, and bring them to their own land. And I will make them one nation in the land, on the mountains of Israel. And one king shall be king over them all, and they shall be no longer two nations, and no longer divided into two kingdoms. They shall not defile themselves anymore with their idols and their detestable things, or with any of their transgressions. But I will save them from all the backslidings in which they have sinned, and will cleanse them; and they shall be my people, and I will be their God. My servant David shall be king over them, and they shall all have one shepherd. They shall walk in my rules and be careful to obey my statutes. They shall dwell in the land that I gave to my servant Jacob, where your fathers lived. They and their children and their children's children shall dwell there forever, and David my servant shall be their prince forever" (Ezek 37:21–25).

- "In that day, declares the LORD, I will assemble the lame and gather those who have been driven away and those whom I have afflicted; and the lame I will make the remnant, and those who were cast off, a strong nation; and the LORD will reign over them in Mount Zion from this time forth and forevermore. And you, O tower of the flock, hill of the daughter of Zion, to you shall it come, the former dominion shall come, kingship for the daughter of Jerusalem" (Mic 4:6–8).

(d) Immanuel's kingdom shall extend to the nations in the earth.

- "May all kings fall down before him, all nations serve him! May his name endure forever, his fame continue as long as the sun! May people be blessed in him, all nations call him blessed" (Ps 72:11, 17).

- "All the nations you have made shall come and worship before you, O Lord, and shall glorify your name" (Ps 86:9).

- "Behold, you shall call a nation that you do not know, and a nation that did not know you shall run to you, because of the LORD your God, and of the Holy One of Israel, for he has glorified you" (Isa 55:5)

- "I saw in the night visions, and behold, with the clouds of heaven there came one like a son of man, and he came to the Ancient of Days and was presented before him. And to him was given dominion and glory and a kingdom, that all peoples, nations, and languages should serve him; his dominion is an everlasting dominion, which shall not pass away, and his kingdom one that shall not be destroyed" (Dan 7:13–14).

- "And many nations shall come, and say: 'Come, let us go up to the mountain of the LORD, to the house of the God of Jacob, that he may teach us his ways and that we may walk in his paths.' For out of Zion shall go forth the law, and the word of the LORD from Jerusalem" (Mic 4:2).

- "Many peoples and strong nations shall come to seek the LORD of hosts in Jerusalem and to entreat the favor of the LORD" (Zech 8:22).

- "'I will plant them on their land, and they shall never again be uprooted out of the land that I have given them,' says the LORD your God" (Amos 9:15).

Immanuel's kingdom will be established by the power of the returning King.

- "Then the LORD your God will restore your fortunes and have mercy on you, and he will gather you again from all the peoples where the LORD your God has scattered you" (Deut 30:3).

- "Our God comes; he does not keep silence; before him is a devouring fire, around him a mighty tempest. He calls to the heavens above and to the earth, that he may judge his people: 'Gather to me my faithful ones, who made a covenant with me by sacrifice'" (Ps 50:3–5).

- "For he comes, for he comes to judge the earth. He will judge the world in righteousness, and the peoples in his faithfulness" (Ps 96:13).

- "Sing and rejoice, O daughter of Zion, for behold, I come and I will dwell in your midst, declares the LORD. And many nations shall join themselves to the LORD in that day, and shall be my people. And I will dwell in your midst, and you shall know that the LORD of hosts has sent me to you. And the LORD will inherit Judah as his portion in the holy land, and will again choose Jerusalem. Be silent, all flesh, before the LORD, for he has roused himself from his holy dwelling" (Zech 2:10–12).

- "Behold, I send my messenger, and he will prepare the way before me. And the Lord whom you seek will suddenly come to his temple; and the messenger of the covenant in whom you delight, behold, he is coming, says the LORD of hosts. But who can endure the day of his coming, and who can stand when he appears? For he is like a refiner's fire and like fullers' soap. He will sit as a refiner and purifier of silver, and he will purify the sons of Levi and refine them like gold and silver, and they will bring offerings in righteousness to the LORD. Then the offering of Judah and Jerusalem will be pleasing to the LORD as in the days of old and as in former years" (Mal 3:1–4).

Immanuel's kingdom will be spiritual.

Not incorporeal, or separate from that which is material; but spiritual in that the will of God will be directly effective in all matters of government and conduct. The joy and blessedness of fellowship with God will be experienced by all. The political, temporal kingdom will be conducted in perfect righteousness and true holiness. The kingdom of God will again be "in the midst" (Luke 17:21) in the Person of the Messiah King and He will rule in the grace and power of the sevenfold Spirit (Isa 11:2–3). Judah shall be saved, and Israel shall dwell safely, and the nations shall walk in the light of God. "Many peoples and strong nations shall come to seek the LORD of hosts in Jerusalem and to entreat the favor of the LORD." The trees of the field shall clap their hands for joy. These passages, which might be multiplied many times, may serve to outline the prophet's vision of the features of Messiah's earthly kingdom which was covenanted to David. This kingdom has ever been Israel's only hope and was the consolation for which she waited when Christ was born (Luke 2:25).

4

The Kingdom Offered

In subject matter the division between the Old Testament and the New occurs at the cross of Christ, rather than between Malachi and Matthew. The Gospels, in the main, carry forward the same dispensational conditions that were in effect at the hour when Christ was born. Especially is this true of the Gospel of Matthew, Christ being set forth in that Gospel, first of all, as a King with His kingdom in full view. The Spirit has faithfully selected those deeds and teachings of Christ from the complete manifestation in the flesh which portray Him in the dominant character reflected in each Gospel. In Matthew He is presented as the King; in Mark as Jehovah's servant; in Luke as the perfect human; and in John as the very Son of God. In all these narratives, this one Person is seen acting and teaching under the same conditions which existed for centuries before the cross. There is some anticipation of what would follow the cross as there is reference after the cross to what had gone before. Whatever preceded the cross, in the main, fell under those conditions and colorings of "the law which came by Moses," and Jesus not only held up Moses as the authority for the time, but also expanded his teachings. A great division between the Old Testament and the New, herefore, lies in the fact that "grace and truth came by Jesus Christ," and became effective with the cross of Christ rather than with His birth.

Matthew opens with an emphasis upon Christ as the Son of David: "The book of the generation (*genea*, nationality or line of descent, cf. Matt 24:34) of Jesus Christ, the Son of David, the Son of Abraham." Although, in this Gospel, Jesus is presented as the "Son of Abraham" in sacrificial death, the primary purpose of the writer is to set forth the nation's King. This being the only office that is ever assigned to a "Son of David." The tracing of the divinely appointed kingdom thus proceeds from the Old Testament into the New without a change other than the appearance of the long expected King, accompanied by His forerunner, whose predicted ministry had occupied the closing words of the Old Testament revelation. There is no break in the narrative.

The fact that Jesus was David's Greater Son, the fulfiller of all the nation's kingdom blessings is not based on human opinion. It was announced by the angel Gabriel before the birth of Christ as recorded in Luke 1:31–33:

> "And behold, you will conceive in your womb and bear a son, and you shall call his name Jesus. He will be great and will be called the Son of the Most High. And the Lord God will give to him the throne of his father David, and he will reign over the house of Jacob forever, and of his kingdom there will be no end."

This treats distinctly of the "Throne of David" over the "House of Jacob," and proclaims of this kingdom that "there shall be no end." No Gentile blessings are in view here; nor need the Gentiles seek to intrude. Gentile blessings will eventually flow out of this very throne; but these are not in view, nor are any Gentile blessings endangered by a faithful recognition of this distinctly Jewish purpose. The same is clearly stated in Romans 15:8: "For I tell you that Christ became a servant to the circumcised to show God's truthfulness, in order to confirm the promises given to the patriarchs."

He did not come to *annul* those promises; but He did come to *confirm* them. The promises made unto the fathers are well defined: no promises were made to Gentiles. The term "the fathers" can mean none other than God's chosen men of Israel. By these promises Israel was to be redeemed and placed in her own land and that by Immanuel who should be the final Prophet, Priest and King. He should be her King over her covenanted kingdom. These promises made unto the fathers were the nation's only hope, as is clearly indicated: "We trusted that it had been he which should have redeemed Israel." "Lord, wilt thou at this time restore again the kingdom unto Israel?"

In Christ, then, the kingdom covenant made to David had its confirmation as well, it being one of the promises made unto the fathers. How certainly that covenant must stand today!

It is recorded of Jesus that He was "born King of the Jews" (Matt 2:2). To this throne He made final claim at His trial (Matt 27:11). And under this accusation He suffered (Matt 27:29) and died (Matt 27:37). One needs only to search the Scriptures to discover the fact that He is never mentioned as King of the church, nor King of the nations until He comes again as "King of kings, and Lord of lords" (Rev 19:16). He fulfilled every prediction that described Israel's Messiah King and the manner of His coming, at a time when all the records and genealogies were intact. He came of the tribe of Judah, a Son of David, born of a virgin in Bethlehem of Judea. Such claims could not then be made by an impostor without arousing the violent opposition of the rulers of the nation. His claim to be King was never challenged, so far as title was concerned. He met every prediction concerning Israel's Immanuel King. He was that King.

Four centuries before the birth of Jesus Malachi had prophesied the coming of a forerunner to the King:

> "Behold, I will send you Elijah the prophet before the
> great and awesome day of the LORD comes. And he will
> turn the hearts of fathers to their children and the hearts
> of children to their fathers, lest I come and strike the land
> with a decree of utter destruction" (Mal 4:5–6).

This had a certain fulfillment in John the Baptist according, again, to angelic testimony:

> "But the angel said to him, 'Do not be afraid, Zechariah,
> for your prayer has been heard, and your wife Elizabeth

will bear you a son, and you shall call his name John. And
you will have joy and gladness, and many will rejoice at his
birth, for he will be great before the Lord. And he must
not drink wine or strong drink, and he will be filled with
the Holy Spirit, even from his mother's womb. And he
will turn many of the children of Israel to the Lord their
God, and he will go before him in the spirit and power of
Elijah, to turn the hearts of the fathers to the children, and
the disobedient to the wisdom of the just, to make ready
for the Lord a people prepared'" (Luke 1:13–17).

Thus also another Messianic claim was met in the faithful ministry of
John.

The first message of this divinely foreseen witness is recorded thus:
"In those days John the Baptist came preaching in the wilderness of
Judea, 'Repent, for the kingdom of heaven is at hand'" (Matt 3:1–2).
This, too, was the first message recorded of Christ: "From that time Jesus
began to preach, saying, 'Repent, for the kingdom of heaven is at hand'"
(Matt 4:17). So, again, it was the only message committed to His disciples
when He first sent them forth to preach: "These twelve Jesus sent out,
instructing them, 'Go nowhere among the Gentiles and enter no town of
the Samaritans, but go rather to the lost sheep of the house of Israel. And
proclaim as you go, saying, "The kingdom of heaven is at hand"'" (Matt
10:5–7). This message, it will be seen, had no application to Gentiles:
The messengers were to go only "to the lost sheep of the house of Israel."
It can scarcely be unnoticed that while every detail of the manner of their
journey was subject to the most careful instruction by the King, there is
no record of instruction having been given them as to the meaning of this
first, or kingdom, message committed to them. Evidently they did not
need such instruction concerning the kingdom. Had not the kingdom
hope been passed from father to son for generations? Had it not been
sung to them at their mother's knee? Had it not been the one great theme
of the synagogue instruction? Was it not their national hope? How much
in contrast to this was the prolonged inability on the part of these same

disciples to grasp, later on, the new message and world-wide commission of the cross!

This focusing of the testimony of Jesus, of John and of the disciples upon one solitary message, "The kingdom of heaven is at hand," places that message under unusual emphasis and its actual meaning should be carefully considered.

The phrase "kingdom of heaven" is found only in Matthew, the Gospel of the King, and there it appears with different shades of meaning. One only of these shades of meaning is used in Chapters 1 to 12 of this Gospel. Here it seems to refer to the same earthly Davidic kingdom with which the Old Testament had closed. As has been stated, whatever was meant by this announcement of the "kingdom of heaven," it was clearly understood by the preachers who proclaimed it and by the hearers.

No other kingdom message could have thus been received by those people in that day. So, also, it was addressed to one nation, Israel, and to them as a whole, rather than to individuals. Thus the "kingdom of heaven" as a message must ever be distinguished from the message of the gospel of grace which came by the cross. The gospel of grace Israel, as a nation, has never understood, and it is addressed to all peoples and to them as individuals only. The message of the "kingdom of heaven" as first set forth by Matthew had, therefore, a limited and national meaning—limited as to time of its application, because a new message has come in; and national, because, for the time being, it was addressed to Israel alone.

The message of the "kingdom of heaven" did not concern itself so much with the Person of the King as it did with His kingdom. But Israel had never dreamed of a kingdom apart from the presence and power of the expected King. Thus Jesus could say of Himself, in the light of the accepted close relation between the Person of the King and His kingdom: "The kingdom of God is in the midst of you" ("in the midst," in the Person of the King, Luke 17:21). To assert the imminency of the kingdom was, to them, to assert the imminency of the King.

This kingdom message conforms in another respect, also, to the conditions of the Old Testament kingdom. There must be a great national heart-turning, or repentance to God as an immediate preparation for the kingdom as seen in the Old Testament (Deut 30:1–3; Isa 24:7; Hos 3:4, 5; 14:7; Zech 12:10–13:1; Mal 3:7). Repentance, therefore, became an imperative part of the message concerning the imminency of the kingdom. So each of these kingdom messengers called upon that nation to repent: a "brood of vipers" must "bear fruits in keeping with repentance." They must turn about in heart as a condition of this covenanted kingdom blessing. This they, by His grace, are yet to do, "in His time." It is to be regretted that this required national repentance of Israel has been so often misapplied as a necessary preliminary step in an individual's salvation by Grace.

As certainly as the message of the "kingdom of heaven" was a claim upon the nation's hope, so, also, the rule of life presented in connection with this claim by both John the Baptist and Christ was in harmony with the Old Testament kingdom rule of life. The kingdom as foreseen in the Old Testament had ever in view the righteousness in life and conduct of its subjects (Isa 11:3–5; 32:1; Jer 23:6; Dan 9:24). The "kingdom of heaven" as announced and offered in the early part of Matthew's Gospel is also accompanied with positive demands for personal righteousness in life and conduct. This is not the principle of grace: it is rather the principle of law. It extends into finer detail the law of Moses; but it never ceases to be the very opposite of the principle of grace. Law conditions its blessings on human works: Grace conditions its works on divine blessings. Law says: "If you forgive, you will be forgiven," and in that measure only (Matt 6:14–15): while grace says: "Forgiving one another, as God in Christ forgave you" (Eph 4:32). So, again, law says: "Unless your righteousness exceeds that of the scribes and Pharisees, you will never enter the kingdom of heaven" (Matt 5:20). This is not a present condition for entrance into heaven. Present conditions are wholly based on mercy: "He saved us, not because of works done by us in righteousness, but according to his own mercy" (Titus 3:5). So the preaching of John the Baptist, like the Sermon on the Mount, was on a law basis as indicated by its appeal which was only for a correct and righteous life:

He said therefore to the crowds that came out to be baptized by him, "You brood of vipers! Who warned you to flee from the wrath to come?

Bear fruits in keeping with repentance. And do not begin to say to yourselves, 'We have Abraham as our father.' For I tell you, God is able from these stones to raise up children for Abraham. Even now the axe is laid to the root of the trees. Every tree therefore that does not bear good fruit is cut down and thrown into the fire." And the crowds asked him, "What then shall we do?" And he answered them, "Whoever has two tunics is to share with him who has none, and whoever has food is to do likewise." Tax collectors also came to be baptized and said to him, "Teacher, what shall we do?" And he said to them, "Collect no more than you are authorized to do." Soldiers also asked him, "And we, what shall we do?" And he said to them, "Do not extort money from anyone by threats or by false accusation, and be content with your wages" (Luke 3:7–14).

This, like the Sermon on the Mount, is an appeal for a righteous life and cannot be confused with the present terms of salvation without nullifying the grounds of every hope and promise under grace. The present appeal to the unsaved is not for better conduct: it is for personal belief in, and acceptance of, the Savior. There are directions concerning the conduct of those who are saved by trust in the Savior; but these cannot be mixed with the law conditions of the Old Testament, or the New, without peril to souls. Later on the same people said to Christ: "What must we do, to be doing the works of God?" And to this He replied: "This is the work of God, that you believe in him whom he has sent" (John 6:28–29). John the Baptist looked forward to the blessings of grace when he said: "Behold the Lamb of God who takes away the sin of the world;" but his immediate demands were in conformity with pure law, as were the early teachings of Jesus. Thus the legal principles of conduct of the Old Testament kingdom are carried forward into the revelations of the same kingdom as it appears in the New Testament.

The right division of Scripture does not destroy these legal passages; but it does fully classify them with the other Scriptures relating to the kingdom, both in the Old Testament and the New. There are many elements found in this body of truth that indicate the required manner of life in the kingdom which will be found likewise under the consistent walk in grace; but whatever is carried forward to be a life-governing principle under grace is there restated in its own place and with its own new emphasis. Thus the two widely differing systems are meant to be kept distinct in the mind of the faithful student of God's Word.

It should be borne in mind that the legal kingdom requirements as stated in the Sermon on the Mount are meant to prepare the way for, and condition life in, the earthly Davidic kingdom when it shall be set up upon the *earth,* and at that time when the kingdom prayer, "Your kingdom come, your will be done, on earth as it is in heaven," has been answered. These kingdom conditions appear in the early ministry of Jesus since He was at that time faithfully offering the Messianic kingdom to Israel.

It has been objected that such stipulations as "resist not evil;" "if one shall smite you on the one cheek;" "one shall compel you to go a mile;" and "persecutions for righteousness' sake," could not be possible in the kingdom. This challenge may be based upon a supposition that the earthly Messianic kingdom is to be as morally perfect as heaven. On the contrary, the Scriptures abundantly testify that, while there will be far less occasion to sin, for the sufficient reason that Satan is then bound and in a pit and the glorious King is on His throne, there will be need of immediate execution of judgment and justice in the earth, and even the King shall rule, of necessity, with a "rod of iron." It is said that "all Israel shall be saved" and "all shall know the Lord from the least even unto the greatest;" but it is also revealed that at the end of that millennium, when Satan is loosed for a little season, he is still able to solicit the allegiance of human hearts and to draw out of the multitudes within the kingdom an army for rebellion against the government of the King (Rev 20:7–9). In that kingdom age "the sinner a hundred years old shall be accursed" (Isa 65:20). The saints of that age will doubtless have heaven before their eyes and be looking there for their reward. And they will be the "salt of the earth."

These kingdom commands and principles were given to Israel only and it is that same distinct nation that shall stand first in that kingdom when it is set up in the earth. Jesus was first "a minister to the circumcision," and is it an unnatural interpretation of Scripture to understand that He was performing this divinely appointed ministry at that very time when He was offering the kingdom to that nation and when He, with His forerunner, was depicting the principles of conduct that should condition life in that kingdom? Nothing is lost by such an interpretation; on the contrary, everything is gained, for the riches of grace, which, alas, so few apprehend, are thus kept pure and free from an unscriptural mixture with the kingdom law.

It may be concluded that the term "kingdom of heaven" as used in the early ministry of Jesus referred to the Messianic, Davidic, earthly kingdom seen in the Old Testament. As has been noted, the Jewish preachers needed no instruction in the details of that message. It was the hope of their nation, and it was addressed to that nation alone. So, also, an appeal was made with this message for the anticipated national, repentance which must precede the setting up of their kingdom in the earth, and the requirements set forth were legal rather than gracious. Israel's kingdom was faithfully offered to them by their King at His first appearing.

5

The Kingdom Rejected and Postponed

The fact that the other Gospels present certain revelations as related to the kingdom of God which Matthew has related to the kingdom of heaven has been accepted by some as grounds for concluding that these terms are synonymous. There can be no question that there is much in common between whatever may be represented by these two terms, else they would not be used interchangeably. The common ground between them lies, it would seem, in the fact that both refer to a certain divine authority, or government. A study of the passages involved will reveal that there is a wide difference between the kingdom of God and the kingdom of heaven. This will be seen to be in the extent of government which is implied in each. The term "kingdom of God," it will be found, is employed when there is nothing stated that would limit its authority over all the universe. The term "kingdom of heaven," it will also be found, is used when the divine government is considered as limited to the earth. There is an important difference, as well, in the possible moral character of each. It is not said of the kingdom of God, as it is of the kingdom of heaven, that there are divine judgments required for wrongdoers within its bounds, or that the false wheat, or tares, and bad fish are a part of it. Entrance into the kingdom of heaven, in its Messianic form, may be by so low a standard as that which merely exceeds the righteousness of the Scribes and the Pharisees (Matt 5:20): while entrance into the kingdom of God is by a new birth alone (John 3:3). The kingdom of heaven is the divine government in the earth which passes through changing phases until every foe has been conquered, and it is finally merged, perfected, into the all-inclusive kingdom of God (1 Cor 15:24–28). For this final consummation we plead when we pray: "Your kingdom come. Your will be done on earth, as it is in heaven." Whatever within this divine government in the earth is consonant with the perfect character of the kingdom of God may be considered as a part of that kingdom; though some of its subjects, who are perfect in standing, may be quite imperfect in life and conduct.

The kingdom of heaven has been defined by Revelation C. I. Scofield, D. D., in the *Scofield Reference Bible* thus:

(1) The phrase, kingdom of heaven (lit, of the heavens), is peculiar to Matthew and signifies the Messianic earth rule of Jesus Christ, the Son of David. It is called the kingdom of heaven because it is the rule of the heavens over the earth (Matt 6:10). The phrase is derived from Daniel, where it is defined (Dan 2:34–36, 44; 7:23–27) as the kingdom which 'the God of heaven' will set up after the destruction by the 'stone cut out without hands' of the Gentile world-system. It is the kingdom covenanted to David's seed (2 Sam 7:7–10); described in the prophets (Zech 12:8, note); and confirmed to Jesus Christ, the Son of Mary, through the angel Gabriel (Luke 1:32, 33).

(2) The kingdom of heaven has three aspects in Matthew: (a) 'at hand' from the beginning of the ministry of John the Baptist (Matt 3:2) to the virtual rejection of the King, and the announcement of the new brotherhood (Matt 12:46–50); (b) In seven 'mysteries of the kingdom of heaven,' to be fulfilled during the present age (Matt 13:1–52), to which are to be added the parables of the kingdom of heaven which were spoken after those of Matthew 13, and which have to do with the sphere of Christian profession during this age; (c) The prophetic aspect—the kingdom to be set up after the return of the

King in glory (Matt 24:29–25:46; Luke 19:12–19; Acts 15:14–17).—*Scofield Reference Bible*, page 996.

So, again, the kingdom of God is to be distinguished from the kingdom of heaven in five respects (cf. Matt 3:2, note):

(1) The kingdom of God is universal, including all moral intelligence willingly subject to the will of God, whether angels, the Church, or saints of past or future dispensations (Luke 13:28, 29; Heb 12:22, 23); while the kingdom of heaven is Messianic, Mediatorial, Davidic, and has for its object the establishment of the kingdom of God in the earth (Matt 3:2, note; 1 Cor 15:24, 25).

(2) The kingdom of God is entered only by the new birth (John 3:3, 5–7); the kingdom of heaven, during this age, is the sphere of a profession which may be real or false (Matt 13:3, note; 25:1, 11, 12).

(3) Since the kingdom of heaven is the earthly sphere of the universal kingdom of God, the two have almost all things in common. For this reason many parables and other teachings are spoken of the kingdom of heaven in Matthew, and of the kingdom of God in Mark and Luke. It is the omissions which are significant. The parables of the wheat and tares, and of the net (Matt 13:24–30, 36–43, 47–50) are not spoken of the kingdom of God. In that kingdom there are neither tares nor bad fish. But the parable of the leaven (Matt 13:33) is spoken of the kingdom of God also, for, alas, even the true doctrines of the kingdom are leavened with the errors of which the Pharisees, Sadducees, and Herodians were the representatives. (See Matt 13:33, note.)

(4) The kingdom of God 'comes not with outward show' (Luke 17:20), but is chiefly that which is inward and spiritual (Rom 14:17); while the kingdom of heaven is organic, and is to be manifested in glory on the earth...

(5) The kingdom of heaven merges into the kingdom of God when Christ, having 'put all enemies under His feet,' 'shall have delivered up the kingdom to God, even the Father' (1 Cor 15:24–28).—*Scofield Reference Bible*, page 1003.

The various uses of the term "kingdom of heaven" in Matthew's Gospel represent the progressive stages through which the government of God in the earth must pass in arriving at the determined end. The first use of the term is in connection with the offer of a kingdom to Israel which had been covenanted to David and described by the prophets of the Old Testament and that which forms the hope of Israel to this hour. This offer of the kingdom which was extended through Christ, John, and the disciples to the nation was rejected by that nation, notwithstanding the fact that it was in complete fulfillment of every divinely given prediction. It was a bona fide offer and, had they received Him as their King, the nation's hope would have been realized. However, it was in the perfect councils and foreknowledge of God that the offer would be rejected, and thereby the way was made for the realization of the great unrevealed purpose of God, which was to be accomplished before the final manifestation of the kingdom in the earth.

This first offer of the kingdom had been typified by the events at Kadesh-Barnea. There this same nation, which had already tasted the discomforts of the desert, were given an opportunity to immediately enter their promised land. Thus left to choose, they failed to enter, and returned to forty years more of wilderness wandering and added judgments. They might have entered the land in blessing. God knew they would not; still it was through their own choice that the blessing was postponed. Later they were brought again to the land after their judgments and afflictions in the wilderness. This time, however, it was without reference to their own choice. With the high hand of Jehovah God they were placed in their own land. So Israel, already five hundred years out of the land, and without a king, rejected the King and the kingdom as offered in Christ, and still continues the wilderness afflictions among all the nations of the earth whither the Lord God hath driven them. But He will yet regather them, else the oath of Jehovah will fail, and that regathering will be without reference to their own choosing, or merit. Under an unconditional covenant He has pledged to place them in kingdom blessings, under the glorious reign of their Immanuel King and in their own land (Deut 30:3–5; Isa 11:10–13; Jer 23:3–8; Ezek 37:21–25). This, too, shall be done by no human processes, but by the mighty power of God.

The first evidence of Israel's rejection of her kingdom as offered by her King is seen in the record that John the Baptist had been placed in prison (Matt 11:2). What could the imprisonment of the forerunner mean other than a step toward the rejection of the King? Immediately the King utters His first words of judgment and doom:

> "Then he began to denounce the cities where most of his mighty works had been done, because they did not repent. 'Woe to you, Chorazin! Woe to you, Bethsaida! For if the mighty works done in you had been done in Tyre and Sidon, they would have repented long ago in sackcloth and ashes. But I tell you, it will be more bearable on the day of judgment for Tyre and Sidon than for you. And you, Capernaum, will you be exalted to heaven? You will be brought down to Hades. For if the mighty works done in you had been done in Sodom, it would have remained until this day. But I tell you that it will be more tolerable on the day of judgment for the land of Sodom than for you'" (Matt 11:20–24).

Chorazin, Bethsaida and Capernaum were the cities in which He had given greatest proof of His Messiahship and they were therefore most guilty in His rejection.

In connection with this first evidence of rejection there is introduced a note wholly foreign to the kingdom theme, and with great significance: "Come to me, all who labor and are heavy laden, and I will give you rest" (Matt 11:28). Everything is in contrast: this is not an offer of a kingdom to a nation, but of soul rest to the individual who will come to Him. A rest which results from coming to know the Father through the Son (Matt 11:27), whom to know aright is eternal life (John 17:3). The reality contained in this offer could only be realized by His cross. Christ was evidently associating, even then, His rejection with His cross. It was as though He was comforting His own heart with a moment's reflection upon the "joy that was set before him" for which He would "endure the cross and despise the shame." Who shall measure the joy of His heart in bringing rest to one sin-sick soul (Isa 53:11)? This flash-light on the coming redemption by His cross immediately passes and the King continues to present Himself to the nation as their King. He proves again by the mighty works of the following chapter that He is none other than their long looked for Messiah; yet in the midst of these infallible proofs it is recorded: "But the Pharisees went out and conspired against him, how to destroy him" (Matt 12:14). The death of John the Baptist (Matt 14:1–13) is also followed by a rebuke to the Pharisees and by words of judgment upon them (Matt 15:1–20).

Another glance forward toward His cross is recorded in connection with His evident rejection in Matthew 16:13–18:

> "Now when Jesus came into the district of Caesarea Philippi, he asked his disciples, 'Who do people say that the Son of Man is?' And they said, 'Some say John the Baptist, others say Elijah, and others Jeremiah or one of the prophets.' He said to them, 'But who do you say that I am?' Simon Peter replied, 'You are the Christ, the Son of the living God.' And Jesus answered him, 'Blessed are you,

Simon Bar-Jonah! For flesh and blood has not revealed
this to you, but my Father who is in heaven. And I tell you,
you are Peter, and on this rock I will build my church, and
the gates of hell shall not prevail against it.'"

The rejection is seen in the report of the disciples that Christ was
accounted for by the men of the nation to whom He had come as being
John the Baptist, Elias, Jeremias, or one of the prophets.

How impressed they were with His Personality and power! Yet how
preposterous that He should be confused with John with whom He had
so recently stood among them! They were evidently willing to account
for Him by any subterfuge that would relieve them of the acknowledg-
ment of Him as their King. In connection with this new evidence of
rejection He again reflects upon the joy that was to be His through His
cross: "On this rock I will build my church." The church, His precious
bride, which He loved and for which He gave Himself; "that he might
sanctify her, having cleansed her by the washing of water with the word,
so that he might present the church to himself in splendor, without
spot or wrinkle or any such thing, that she might be holy and without
blemish" (Eph 5:26–27). This, again, is the joy that was set before Him
and which would be realized only by His rejection and sacrificial death.

Continuing the narrative of the Gospel of the King to its end, He is
seen still offering Himself to the nation as their King, riding meek and
lowly into Jerusalem that the Scriptures might be fulfilled, and dying
under the fatal and final claim to be the "King of the Jews." Along
with this is the record of the ever increasing animosity and rejection
of the nation, leading up to the climacteric expression of their hatred,
the crucifixion of their King between two thieves. Thus the supreme
wickedness of man descended to its lowest depths of sin against God; yet
by this death the flood-gates of life were opened and the very sin of His
crucifixion was laid back upon His own breast, as He met all the doom
that must fall upon "the Lamb of God who takes away the sin of the
world."

When the nation began to reject her King, He not only began to anticipate His sacrificial death and the blessings to flow out of it, but He began, also, to speak of returning to this earth again, and to associate the realization of His earthly kingdom with that event. That the kingdom was to be realized through a return of the divine Person was certainly in the foreknowledge of God and was foretold by prophets (Deut 30:3; Dan 7:13, 14). However, in the main, the prophets did not distinguish the fulfilling of the Lamb, or sacrificial type, in the first advent from the fulfilling of the Lion, or kingly type, in the second advent. On the other hand, by the Spirit, who inspired them, they never confused these great issues, although the time relations that were to exist between these two vastly different ministries of Christ were not revealed to them. Of this Peter writes in 1 Peter 1:10–11 thus: "Concerning this salvation, the prophets who prophesied about the grace that was to be yours searched and inquired carefully, inquiring what person or time the Spirit of Christ in them was indicating when he predicted the sufferings of Christ and the subsequent glories." The unsolved problem was the time intervening between the sufferings of Christ in connection with His first coming, and His manifestation in glory when He should come the second time.

To conclude that these literal earthly blessings for Israel were transferred into spiritual blessings for all nations because Israel rejected and crucified her King at His first appearing, compels one to ignore the bulk of Old Testament prophecies and the plain promises and teachings of Jesus. The oath of Jehovah still stands, and He knows no defeat. His plan has not been changed. To speak of the kingdom as postponed is to consider it within the perspective of Israel's final glory. If the oath, covenant and promises of Jehovah cannot be trusted, what assurance can be drawn from any word He has spoken? Purposing to instruct us as to a yet future earthly kingdom for Israel, and for the nations through them, what more positive, or meaningful, language could He have employed?

6

Present Truth

At least seven realities not seen by the Old Testament writers were brought into view and made possible through the cross. These, with all correlated truth, form the distinct revelation of "grace and truth" that "came by Jesus Christ" and "the New Testament in his blood." Peter writes of this body of Scripture as "present truth" (2 Pet 1:12), doubtless from the fact that it sets forth the divine blessings and relationships which are obviously effective within the present age. These new unfoldings of "grace and truth," it will be seen, are in no way related to, or a part of, those earthly kingdom revelations which had been previously recorded by the sacred writers. Much is in contrast between these two bodies of truth; but it is even more important to see that a great difference lies in the fact that one treats of a celestial sphere of spiritual reality which is as much above the temporal, earthly covenants of the other as heaven is higher than the earth.

These new conditions flowing from, and made possible by, the cross are not a readjustment of defeated Old Testament purposes, or the merging of the old order into the new. What was purposed in the earthly kingdom is still following its own divine order and development to its own mighty consummation. Its present form is exactly what God intended it to be at this hour, and all this will lead as certainly to the fulfillment of every predicted manifestation in the earth. Christianity is totally opposite to Judaism and any mixture of the two must result in the loss of all that is vital in the present plan of Salvation. One made its appeal to the limited resources of the natural man and conditioned his life on the earth: the other sets aside the natural man, secures a whole new creation in Christ Jesus, and counsels that new being in his pilgrim journey to his heavenly, home. Israel's kingdom revelation, dealing with the past or present, does not gather into itself the distinct relationships that form the elements of "present truth," which are for this age only. On the other hand, the kingdom realization awaits the return of the King. The prolonged dispersions of Israel among the nations, with the divine preservation of that people, is not only clearly anticipated in Scripture (Hos 3:4, 5; Luke 21:24; Rom 11:25; Acts 15:13–18; Luke 19:11–13), but is one of the most evident facts of history. With the Gentile world opposing the Jew, at times bent upon their extermination, behold them now! Although comparatively few in number, they are rapidly rising to the place of command among the peoples of earth in finance, in the professions, in science and the fine arts. What this augurs to the devout student of Jewish prophecy is obvious.

The new issues, growing out of the cross, which confront the Bible student are the following.

1. Life from God through a new birth by the Spirit.

What relation to God was accorded to Old Testament saints is not clearly revealed. Doubtless they were individually renewed by the Spirit as they came to believe in God for their personal salvation. Whatever may have been the result of their spiritual change, they knew nothing of a new life and sonship as it is set forth in the New Testament. Nicodemus, than whom the nation could then produce no better, and representing the very highest product of the "Jew's religion," needed to be told that even he "must be born again." So foreign was this to his knowledge of truth that he could only reply: "How can these things be?" Paul, who had lived "in all good conscience" within the revelations of the nation's faith, must be transformed into a new creature on the Damascus road. After this he ceased not to pray for like members of his own nation who had a "zeal for God" that they, too, might be saved. One passage upon this point may be sufficient:

But when the fullness of time had come, God sent forth his Son, born of woman, born under the law, to redeem those who were under the law, so that we might receive adoption as sons. And because you are sons, God has sent the Spirit of his Son into our hearts, crying, "Abba! Father!" So you are no longer a slave, but a son, and if a son, then an heir through God (Gal 4:4–7).

The new life by the Spirit is presented in the Scriptures as the fundamental and distinguishing fact of the Christian. Upwards of a hundred New Testament passages emphasize this truth. In these passages a "new creation," or species, is said to be formed by the mighty creative power of God (Eph 2:10). This newly created one is not of this earth, but is a citizen of heaven (Phil 3:20). He is a legitimate son of God by a legitimate birth through the Spirit (John 3:6); possessing the divine nature (2 Pet 1:4), which is eternal life through Jesus Christ our Lord (Rom 3:23). Being properly a son of God, he is said to be an heir of God and a joint-heir with Jesus Christ (Rom 8:17; Gal 4:7).

God alone is sufficient for the miracles that together produce a Christian, and the reasonableness of the way of salvation is seen in that it must be received as a gift and on the basis of trusting Him for its accomplishment. This fact of regeneration is the only present issue between God and an unsaved person. When this is accomplished the obviously desirable reformation in life and conduct will be outwardly manifested by the new inwrought divine nature and power.

How short the vision is which can see no farther than to strive for the reformation of an individual in matters of purpose and conduct, as desirable as such reformation may be, when the divine plan to produce a whole new being with its new heart, disposition and power is so plainly revealed! It is puerile to be obsessed with a by-product of the fact of eternal life. Certainly this is not an abstract issue: having passed from death unto life has been, and will be, the abiding miracle in the life of individuals of all generations from the cross of Christ until He comes again. As certainly, also, such efforts toward reformation cannot be justified from Scripture; for interpretations which would suggest conduct to be the primary issue between God and the unsaved cannot be found unless Israel's law is borrowed, or the humanly impossible walk of the regenerate is imposed upon the unregenerate.

2. A new standing.

It was never said of any Old Testament saint that he was "a member of the body of Christ," or that he was "accepted in the beloved;" but the New Testament saint is all this, and has been "made the righteousness of God in him" (Rom 3:21–22; 10:3, 4; 1 Cor 1:30; 2 Cor 5:21; Eph 1:6).

3. A new sufficiency.

As truly as the Christian is a new creature and a heavenly citizen, so every condition within the new life is supernatural. The human limitation has been perfectly anticipated and provided for in the fact that the all-sufficient Spirit indwells every saved person (Rom 5:5; 8:9; John 3:6; 7:39; 14:16, 17; Gal 6:4; 1 Cor 6:19). This universal abiding presence of the Spirit in a saved person, providing nothing short of the sufficiency of God for the least of His children, is a vastly different relationship than had been known before (John 7:37–39).

4. A new service.

Service, in the Old Testament, consisted largely in going into the temple, or tabernacle, to offer a sacrifice for sin: in the New Testament it is going out to the uttermost parts of the earth to witness to a perfect sacrifice fully accomplished. The former had self with its personal needs in view: the latter has found rest for self, and from self, and moves out to others in the mighty empowering "gifts of the Spirit."

5. A new rule of life.

The epistles of the New Testament present a distinct heavenly rule of life which is gracious in contrast to law. They instruct a heavenly citizen in his normal walk and life. Attempted obedience to these precepts will never make a heavenly citizen: they are rather set before him because he is already a heavenly citizen through the power of God. Therefore they do not carry a legal imperative; but are presented as "beseechings," and under the suggestive phrase, "as it becometh saints." The law was given to Israel alone and only when she had been redeemed out of Egypt. The law of Moses did not redeem Israel: it became her rule of life after she was redeemed. That redemption out of Egypt anticipates, in type, the blood redemption of the cross. So, also, a new governing rule of life is given to those who are looking back in saving faith to Calvary. Obedience to the new principle of life under grace would not save one. It only suggests the normal manner of life for those who have already become heavenly in being through the alone sufficient power of God. The new principle of life through grace is superhuman (Eph 4:1–3, 30; 5:18–22; 2 Cor 10:4, 5; 1 Pet 2:9, etc.); but according to the purpose of God it is to be perfectly fulfilled by the power of the indwelling Spirit (Gal 5:16; Rom 8:2). The law said, "Love your neighbor as yourself" (Lev 18:18; Matt 19:19; 22:39; Rom 13:9; Gal 5:14; James 2:8). Jesus said, "A new commandment I give to you, that you love one another: just as I have loved you, you also are to love one another" (John 13:34; cf. 15:12–13). There could not be a more impossible requirement than that we, of ourselves, should love as He has loved us; but such divine love is produced in us by the unhindered Spirit (Rom 5:5; Gal 5:22).

6. A new purpose.

Most evidently God is not now offering an earthly kingdom to any one nation; nor is He saving every individual of all nations. There is a process of selection going on (if it be held that God is now accomplishing His own will), and, while the Gospel might be preached to all, there is no evidence from history that all who have heard it have been saved, or teaching in the Scripture that all would be saved. God is seen to be dealing with individuals, both Jews and Gentiles, and in such a manner that each one thus dealt with is to be finally changed into the image of Christ, and collectively as His body and bride to be forever with Him.

7. A new prospect.

Centuries before the cross the King and His Messianic kingdom was rightfully expected by the nation to whom the manifestation of the King and the establishment of the kingdom had been promised, and this kingdom was still in view when the new revelation concerning the return of Christ was presented. While the promises to Israel are suffering prolonged delay, the heavenly bride is being called out, and unto her is given a new hope and prospect: "The Lord is at hand" (Phil 4:5).

In the light of these seven "present truth" realities we are enabled to recognize how great is the effect of the change from "the law which came by Moses" and "grace and truth which came by Jesus Christ." And when these changed, age-long conditions have run their course we are assured that there will be a return to the legal kingdom grounds and, the exaltation of that nation to whom pertain the covenants and promises.

The last two elements of "present truth" presented above will each in turn be the basis for a further study of kingdom truth.

7

The Church Which is His Body

The new purpose of God in this age is seen to be the out-calling of a heavenly people. They form a part of the kingdom in its present mystery form (Matt 13); but are in no way related to the Messianic earthly kingdom of Israel other than that they, as the bride of the King, will be associated with Him in His reign (Eph 5:29–32; 2 Tim 2:12; Rev 20:6; 21:9–21). The disciples, being Jews, needed no instruction as to the message of the kingdom; but in marked contrast to this they did not once grasp any reference Jesus made to His sacrificial death by which He was to open the flood-gates of the grace of God. Even after His resurrection and forty days of instruction concerning the kingdom of God (Acts 1:3) they questioned Him as to the realization of the nation's hope: "Lord, will you at this time restore the kingdom to Israel?" (Acts 1:6). His reply is suggestive:

> "It is not for you to know times or seasons that the Father
> has fixed by his own authority. But you will receive power
> when the Holy Spirit has come upon you, and you will be
> my witnesses in Jerusalem and in all Judea and Samaria,
> and to the end of the earth" (Acts 1:7–8).

He does not tell them their kingdom is abandoned, or merged into a spiritual conquest of all nations: He plainly infers that every promise of God is still intact; but assigns to them the immediate ministry of the new gospel age. Even this they failed to comprehend; for it was not until

Peter by divine compulsion had first preached the Gospel to Gentiles in Cornelius' house, and Paul and Barnabas had returned to Jerusalem reporting the same out-flowing salvation to Gentiles as had been given to Jews that they were able to grasp the meaning of the new age. This new light came in connection with the deliberations of the first church council, called by the mother church at Jerusalem, and recorded in Acts 15:13–18. The issue before this council was of the present obligation of believers toward circumcision, the sign of Judaism. Any departure from that divinely given sign naturally required a new revelation of the scope and character of the new divine purpose. Apparently the Jewish system was being set aside. The conclusion of this first council is recorded thus:

> "After they finished speaking, James replied, 'Brothers,
> listen to me. Simeon has related how God first visited
> the Gentiles, to take from them a people for his name.
> And with this the words of the prophets agree, just as it
> is written, "After this I will return, and I will rebuild the
> tent of David that has fallen; I will rebuild its ruins, and I
> will restore it, that the remnant of mankind may seek the
> Lord, and all the Gentiles who are called by my name, says
> the Lord, who makes these things known from of old"'"
> (Acts 15:13–18).

There is no more important prophetic Scripture than this because of the arresting fact that it states the present-age purpose of God in relation to the future purposes, and places these in an exact order. The answer to the question of these Jewish Christians as to what was superseding Judaism (the new order having set aside its last distinction, circumcision), is given by James, the pastor of the church in Jerusalem. In this concluding discourse of the council he first states the divine purpose in the new age: "God first [in the house of Cornelius, as Peter had just stated] visited the Gentiles, to take from them a people for his name" (Acts 15:14). The realization of the purpose to gather out a people is to be followed by a "return" of the divine Person to the earth and the reestablishment of the Davidic order, and with this the long awaited world-wide blessing.

The meaning of the word "church" is the "called out ones," and this, it will be seen, is identical with the present-age purpose "to take from them a people for his name." The word "church" appears for the first time in the Bible at Matthew 16:18, and here Jesus speaks of it as a then future thing: "On this rock I *will* build my church." An entirely new word is used, it would seem, that there should be no confusion of what this word represents with any Old Testament revelation.

The general use of the word in the Scriptures is of a collection, or assembly, of people. Thus Israel, separated and called out of Egypt, is termed by Stephen as "the congregation [church] in the wilderness" (Acts 7:38), and Luke uses the same word in mentioning the assembly of people in the town meeting at Ephesus (Acts 19:32). When the word is now used to denote a company of professing Christians, or united worshippers, the reference is to an organization of people of one generation united by human ties, and not all, necessarily, saved ones. The deeper and more important use of the word, however, is the designation of the born-again ones of all generations since Pentecost as "baptized into one body and made to drink of one Spirit," each one so perfectly in the saving and transforming power of God that he will rightfully appear in glory in the exact likeness of Christ; and the whole company, finally perfected, "without spot or wrinkle or any such thing" will be His bride and His body, "the fullness of him who fills all in all."

Such a perfect organism, with its heavenly destiny and glory, could hardly be confused with Israel in the wilderness, called out and separated from Egypt, or the ungovernable assembly of the town meeting at Ephesus, called out for the time being from their homes. The latter are merely incidental: the former is no less than the primary purpose of God in this age of grace.

Little would be known of the out-called heavenly body from the teachings of Jesus, and nothing could be known from any portion of the Old Testament, where it is not once directly mentioned. As recorded, Jesus spoke of the church but three times, and then as something yet to be realized by virtue of His own power; for He said, "I will build my church." That this was a reference to His own body and bride, rather than any local assembly, is evident from His following sentence: "And the gates of hell shall not prevail against it." How woefully they have prevailed against the professing, visible church! Not so, however, against His body and bride.

The fuller revelation of "the church which is his body" (Eph 1:22–23) was committed to the Apostle Paul. Her formation, being and destiny is the theme of the prison revelation and forms the basis of the prison epistles, especially Ephesians and Colossians. The Apostle, writing of this special revelation given to him concerning the purpose of God in this dispensation of grace, records that there was a mystery, or a sacred secret, not made known to other ages, but revealed to himself and the other Apostles that Gentiles were to become fellow heirs with the Jews in one body. A Gentile blessing had been a foreview of the Old Testament and was associated with the earthly kingdom glories of Israel; but Paul's revelation is of a new formation, into a new body, a new creation, "partakers of his promises in Christ by the Gospel," which is not found in the Old Testament. The whole passage is as follows:

> "For this reason I, Paul, a prisoner of Christ Jesus on behalf of you Gentiles—assuming that you have heard of the stewardship of God's grace that was given to me for you, how the mystery was made known to me by revelation, as I have written briefly. When you read this, you can perceive my insight into the mystery of Christ, which was not made known to the sons of men in other generations as it has now been revealed to his holy apostles and prophets by the Spirit. This mystery is that the Gentiles are fellow heirs, members of the same body, and partakers of the promise in Christ Jesus through the gospel. Of this gospel I was made a minister according to the gift of God's grace, which was given me by the working of his power. To me, though I am the very least of all the saints, this grace was given, to preach to the Gentiles the unsearchable riches

of Christ, and to bring to light for everyone what is the plan of the mystery hidden for ages in God, who created all things, so that through the church the manifold wisdom of God might now be made known to the rulers and authorities in the heavenly places. This was according to the eternal purpose that he has realized in Christ Jesus our Lord" (Eph 3:1–11).

From this passage it may be seen that the mystery, or sacred secret, concerning this age was the forming of a new body out of both Jews and Gentiles. This was the "eternal purpose that he has realized in Christ Jesus our Lord."

Preceding this passage, the Apostle has, in Ephesians 2:11–18, not only defined the state of the Gentiles before God, but has made clear that, during this age, all hindrances that might arise from such distinctions have been put away that He might of the two, Jews and Gentiles, make one "new man." "Reconciling both to God in one body through the cross." The two elements of this body, then, are Jews and Gentiles—Gentiles that were "far off," "brought near by the blood of Christ," and Jews that, by covenant, were "near," with Gentiles, "reconciled to God in one body through the cross":

> "Therefore remember that at one time you Gentiles in the flesh, called "the uncircumcision" by what is called the circumcision, which is made in the flesh by hands—remember that you were at that time separated from Christ, alienated from the commonwealth of Israel and strangers to the covenants of promise, having no hope and without God in the world. But now in Christ Jesus you who once were far off have been brought near by the blood of Christ. For he himself is our peace, who has made us both one and has broken down in his flesh the dividing wall of hostility by abolishing the law of commandments expressed in ordinances, that he might create in himself one new man

in place of the two, so making peace, and might reconcile
us both to God in one body through the cross, thereby
killing the hostility. And he came and preached peace to
you who were far off and peace to those who were near.
For through him we both have access in one Spirit to the
Father" (Eph 2:11–18).

The risen and ascended Christ is "head over all things to the church,
which is his body." And they in turn are "the fullness of him who fills all
in all." This is revealed in Ephesians 1:18–23:

"Having the eyes of your hearts enlightened, that you may
know what is the hope to which he has called you, what
are the riches of his glorious inheritance in the saints, and
what is the immeasurable greatness of his power toward us
who believe, according to the working of his great might
that he worked in Christ when he raised him from the
dead and seated him at his right hand in the heavenly
places, far above all rule and authority and power and
dominion, and above every name that is named, not only
in this age but also in the one to come. And he put all
things under his feet and gave him as head over all things
to the church, which is his body, the fullness of him who
fills all in all."

The accomplishment of this age purpose Paul also mentioned in connection with its time relation to the kingdom covenanted to Israel in
Romans 11:25–27:

"Lest you be wise in your own sight, I do not want you to
be unaware of this mystery, brothers: a partial hardening
has come upon Israel, until the fullness of the Gentiles has
come in. And in this way all Israel will be saved, as it is

written, 'The Deliverer will come from Zion, he will banish ungodliness from Jacob; and this will be my covenant
with them when I take away their sins.'"

All this, it will be seen, is in complete accord with the conclusions of
the council at Jerusalem:

> "God first visited the Gentiles, to take from them a people
> for his name. And with this the words of the prophets
> agree, just as it is written, "After this I will return, and I
> will rebuild the tent of David that has fallen; I will rebuild
> its ruins, and I will restore it, that the remnant of mankind
> may seek the Lord, and all the Gentiles who are called by
> my name, says the Lord, who makes these things known
> from of old" (Acts 15:14–17).

This heavenly body is being formed by a process. It had a distinct time
of beginning. It could not have existed before the cross; for it must be
reconciled unto God by that cross. It could not have existed before His
resurrection; for its members must partake of His resurrection life. It
could not have existed before His ascension; for it would have been a
body without its Head (Eph 1:22–23). It could not have existed before
Pentecost; for until then there could have been no organic union by the
baptism of the Spirit into one body (1 Cor 12:13).

"The church which is his body" began to be formed at Pentecost
through the new ministries of the Spirit. Believers, at that time and
through the baptism of the Spirit, became an organism by virtue of a
divine life indwelling all, and that life was Christ. This is fitly illustrated
in Scripture by the figures of the vine and the branches and the head and
the body. One life animates every branch of the vine and every member
of the body:

> "For just as the body is one and has many members, and all the members of the body, though many, are one body, so it is with Christ. For in one Spirit we were all baptized into one body—Jews or Greeks, slaves or free—and all were made to drink of one Spirit. For the body does not consist of one member but of many" (1 Cor 12:12–14).

> "So we, though many, are one body in Christ, and individually members one of another" (Rom 12:5).

> "Because we are members of his body" (Eph 5:30).

Thus the formation of the body began at Pentecost and since that time "the Lord added to their number day by day those who were being saved." It remains to be seen, then, that since the Lord is adding to this body, it is growing, or increasing, unto its perfection during the course of this age. Special ministry gifts, unknown in other ages, are bestowed in this age to serve at divine appointments and in divine power for a limited time, or "*until*" the body is completed:

> "But grace was given to each one of us according to the measure of Christ's gift. Therefore it says, 'When he ascended on high he led a host of captives, and he gave gifts to men.' (In saying, 'He ascended,' what does it mean but that he had also descended into the lower regions, the earth? He who descended is the one who also ascended far above all the heavens, that he might fill all things.) And he gave the apostles, the prophets, the evangelists, the shepherds and teachers, to equip the saints for the work of ministry, for building up the body of Christ, until we all attain to the unity of the faith and of the knowledge of the Son of God, to mature manhood, to the measure of the stature of the fullness of Christ" (Eph 4:7–13).

This, it should be noted, is not the individual perfection of many; but rather the perfection of one body by the adding of many individuals until there is formed "the measure of the stature of the fullness of Christ." The Apostle continues with regard to the growing of this body:

> "Rather, speaking the truth in love, we are to grow up in every way into him who is the head, into Christ, from whom the whole body, joined and held together by every joint with which it is equipped, when each part is working properly, makes the body grow so that it builds itself up in love" (Eph 4:15–16).

So, again, the church is said to be a growing temple eventually to reach its completion, according to another passage in the same Epistle:

> "So then you are no longer strangers and aliens, but you are fellow citizens with the saints and members of the household of God, built on the foundation of the apostles and prophets, Christ Jesus himself being the cornerstone, in whom the whole structure, being joined together, *grows* into a holy temple in the Lord. In him you also are being built together into a dwelling place for God by the Spirit" (Eph 2:19–22).

> "On this rock I will *build* my church" (Matt 16:18).

The outward visible church is not equivalent to "the church which is his body." To that imperfect organization these revelations concerning organic union with Christ and perfection in Christ could hardly be applied.

8

The Bride, The Lamb's Wife

Each of the seven figures used in the New Testament regarding the church suggest some distinct vital relationship between Christ and His heavenly body of people. As sheep they are utterly dependent upon the Shepherd; as branches they draw the vital life from the vine; as stones in a building they rest on the Corner Stone and are mutually dependent on one another; as newly created beings they stand in the

Last Adam, the Head of the new race; as a kingdom of priests they are the objects of intercession of the High Priest and through Him receive their own priestly ministry; as members of His body they are the visible representatives of the Head and the instruments of His manifestation and service; and as the bride of the Lamb they are yet to share in and manifest the ineffable glory and majesty of the Bridegroom-King.

The consummation of the relationships between the Bridegroom and the bride is still to her an anticipation yet to be realized. He has espoused her to Himself: the wedding day awaits His imminent return. It would be normal for her to be looking and longing for His return. Such an attitude is rightly to be expected where any real love for Him exists. His return, however, and the celestial union with His bride will not await the results of the meager power of her poor love for Him. All the divine purpose in calling her out, the present tender grace expended in her behalf, like His certain return, are dependent only on His love for her. This is a love "that surpasses knowledge." Here is sufficient motive to insure the accomplishment of all that the divine wisdom and power can perfect. By no less a perfection will His bride appear in glory. She, because He is able, will be presented faultless before the presence of His glory to His own exceeding joy (Jude 24). That the church is to be His bride and then, as now, the objects of His measureless love, wisdom and power is stated in Ephesians 5:25–32:

> "Husbands, love your wives, as Christ loved the church and gave himself up for her, that he might sanctify her, having cleansed her by the washing of water with the word, so that he might present the church to himself in splendor, without spot or wrinkle or any such thing, that she might be holy and without blemish. In the same way husbands should love their wives as their own bodies. He who loves his wife loves himself. For no one ever hated his own flesh, but nourishes and cherishes it, just as Christ does the church, because we are members of his body. 'Therefore a man shall leave his father and mother and hold fast to his wife, and the two shall become one flesh.' This mystery is profound, and I am saying that it refers to Christ and the church."

In this passage there is a reference to the church as "members of his body." There is also abundant reference to the church as His bride: "I am saying," Paul writes, with reference to husbands and wives, "that it refers to Christ and the church." He loved the church and gave Himself for it that He might present it unto Himself a glorious church. So shall she be "manifested together with him in glory."

The eternal purpose of God in the marvels of His present saving grace is said to be for the realization of these heavenly glories. "He chose us in him before the foundation of the world, that we should be holy and blameless before him" (Eph 1:3). "To the praise of his glorious grace" (Eph 1:6). So again the purpose of God as it sweeps from one eternity to the other is revealed in another Scripture:

> "And raised us up with him and seated us with him in the heavenly places in Christ Jesus, so that in the coming

ages he might show the immeasurable riches of his grace in
kindness toward us in Christ Jesus. For by grace you have
been saved through faith. And this is not your own doing;
it is the gift of God" (Eph 2:6–8).

He hath saved us unto good works, or service (Eph 2:10), and that
we might not perish but have everlasting life (John 3:16): but the passage quoted above seems to indicate that the primary motive of God in
redemption is not to provide that which accrues to man; rather, He is
redeeming His people in order that by them in "the coming ages" He may
display the "riches of his grace" as manifested in "his kindness toward
us in Christ Jesus." When this heavenly people are perfected into the
"measure of the stature of the fullness of Christ," "conformed into his
image," and "like him," it will be a demonstration, before all created
beings, of the marvels of His grace, and upon such a scale and in such
ranges of glory as will wholly satisfy Him. It is His "exceeding joy" that
is in view. Salvation in Christ will manifest His grace; for it is by grace
you are saved. The very purpose of God limits the method by which it
must be done. His purpose is to declare His grace and so salvation is
by grace alone. Where in this marvelous declaration is there any place
for human device or merit? Who would compare this revealed destiny
with any that has ever been imagined by the human mind? Has not
God so stripped man of every self-glorifying moral quality in His sight
that He might, beginning with such utter nothingness, perform and
incomparable display of His unmerited favor and grace?

It is significant that Jesus likened the bride, for whom He gave Himself
that He might purchase her unto Himself, to a pearl of "great cost,"
for which the merchant man sold all that he might possess it. And the
very formation of the pearl is suggestive: It is said that the pearl is built
up, layer upon layer, by the secretions which flow out of the wound in
the side of the shellfish inflicted by the sharp points of the minute grain
of sand lodged under the shell. The pearl, though formed in the triple
darkness of the shell, the mud and the sea, and never having been affected
by the light of the sun, has power when brought up to the light to catch

its rainbow splendor and reflect it back in all its glory. So the church, the "pearl of great cost," is being formed, through the blood that flowed from His riven side, down here in the sea of the nations in this "dark age"; but "what we will be has not yet appeared; but we know that when he appears we shall be like him." The church will then "be to the praise of the glory of his grace." "In the ages to come" showing forth the riches of His grace and glory. "The Lamb is the light thereof."

Referring again to the conclusions of the council at Jerusalem (Acts 15:13–18), it is there stated that a Gentile company is being called out for His name. The "name," when used to designate Deity, seems to carry with it the thought of the Person—"For where two or three are gathered in my name, there am I among them." So this body of people thus called out may be said to be a people for His person. As the bride is for the person of the bridegroom, so the church is for the person of her Lord. This is especially disclosed in John 14:1–3: "Let not your hearts be troubled. Believe in God; believe also in me. In my Father's house are many rooms. If it were not so, would I have told you that I go to prepare a place for you? And if I go and prepare a place for you, I will come again and will take you to myself, that where I am you may be also."

From this passage it will be seen that the bride of the Lamb does not occupy any mansion in the Father's house: He is preparing a place for her and as certainly will come again and receive her, not into the rooms, but unto *Himself*. He loved the church and gave Himself for it that He might purchase it unto *Himself*. "That where I am you may be also." "Father, I desire that they also, whom you have given me, may be with me where I am." "And so we will always be with the Lord." "Who gave himself for us to redeem us from all lawlessness and to purify for himself a people for his own possession who are zealous for good works."

To Israel He is Messiah, Immanuel and King: to the church He is Lord, Head and Bridegroom. The covenants and destinies of Israel are all earthly: the covenants and destinies of the church are all heavenly.

As bride and consort the church will rightfully share with Him His reign (2 Tim 2:12; Rev 5:10; 20:6). The purpose of this age, evidently, is not to form a kingdom by securing subjects of the King; it is the calling out and perfecting into His very image those who will be co-reigners with

Him in His yet future kingdom. The queen is never a subject of the king: her place is to share with him his authority and glory and to rest in the bosom of the bridegroom in the palace of the king.

All the rooms in the Father's house will be occupied. In Hebrews 12:22–24 the inhabitants of heaven are recorded. In this passage it will be noted that there are both "angels" and the "spirits of the righteous made perfect" in addition to "the assembly of the first born":

> "But you have come to Mount Zion and to the city of the living God, the heavenly Jerusalem, and to innumerable angels in festal gathering, and to the assembly of the first-born who are enrolled in heaven, and to God, the judge of all, and to the spirits of the righteous made perfect, and to Jesus, the mediator of a new covenant, and to the sprinkled blood that speaks a better word than the blood of Abel."

Here are seen the redeemed of all ages in heaven; but not all are of the church. The "innumerable angels," and the "spirits of the righteous made perfect" are mentioned as separate from, but accompanying "the assembly of the first born." Here is room for the saints of all the ages who may occupy the "many rooms" without necessarily including the "bride of the Lamb" as undistinguished part of that whole company; for it is said of her, "I go to prepare a place for you." Even John the Baptist, who was certainly of the Old Testament order, must designate himself as "the friend of the bridegroom": "The one who has the bride is the bridegroom. The friend of the bridegroom, who stands and hears him, rejoices greatly at the bridegroom's voice. Therefore this joy of mine is now complete" (John 3:29). Abraham, too, was called "the friend of God" (James 2:23).

A real wedding feast, the feast of the ages, would hardly be attended by the Bridegroom and bride alone. Every element of a feast of such a character we are thus assured will be represented; but it is also clear that one seat will be reserved on His right for His spotless bride. Certainly it is not necessary to conclude that saints of other ages are excluded from heaven, or from the kingdom of God, because they are nowhere represented as organically related to the body and bride of Christ. To merge all the redeemed into one company, or to neglect the distinctions of Scripture, is to do violence to very much of divine revelation.

The church is seen typically, though not directly, in the Old Testament. She, as a royal priesthood, is foreshadowed in the priesthood of the Old Testament; as a new generation, or race, she is the anti-type of that first race which began and fell in Adam; she is the present tabernacle of God, His present abode in the Spirit; she constitutes the true branches of the True Vine; and the sheep that know His voice and will not follow the voice of a stranger. The church is that body formed out of the wound of the side of her living Head, as Eve was formed from Adam.

The bride of Isaac typified the church as did the brides of other marriage unions recorded in the Old Testament. When Isaac was forty years of age, Abraham, fearing lest he might marry some woman of the land, sent his trusted servant, whose name is not given, far away into the old home country to secure a bride for Isaac. When he had made the long journey he was divinely led to select Rebecca to whom that strange offer was to be made. She was asked to go with him, a servant she had never known, to a country she had never seen, to a land from which she would never return, and become the bride of a man she had never met. Truly this was a most unusual request; but she was able to say, "I will go." Then was placed before her some real tokens of Isaac's wealth as foretastes of that inheritance. She decided her future course and lot wholly on the urgent appeal and description given by the unnamed servant of Abraham. They began the long journey back, and she did not know whether to go north, or south, east or west; she must be wholly led by this servant in whom so much confidence had been imposed. As they journeyed during the many days it can be easily believed that he never lost an opportune moment to picture to her new attractions and beauties in the prince Isaac to whom she journeyed. At last she lifted up her eyes and exclaimed with a cry of delight: "Who is that man, walking in the field to meet us?" And the last ministry of that faithful servant was to witness: "It is my master." She sprang down from the beast and ran to meet him and no more blessed marriage union is recorded in all the records of the Old Testament.

God the Father, typified in Abraham in various ways (see Gen 22:1–14), sent the unnamed Servant, the Holy Spirit (the Spirit's name has never been revealed, He is now known only by descriptive titles) to call out a bride for His well-beloved Son. The Servant does not speak of Himself (John 16:13), but glorifies the Son before our eyes, and if we can say: "whom having not seen I love," there is given unto us an earnest of our coming inheritance and glory with Him (2 Cor 1:22; Eph 1:14). How little we then know of our pilgrim journey! But "as many as are led by the Spirit of God they are the sons of God." And while we thus journey that faithful Guide does not cease to unfold the riches of grace and glory that meet in Jesus our Lord (John 16:12–15), and the day is not far away, we believe, when we shall lift our eyes and exclaim, "Who comes yonder?" And the final ministry of our unnamed Guide will be to present us to Him without spot or wrinkle, or any such thing, "and so we will always be with the Lord."

No human thought needs to be added to God's own description of the blessed estate of those He is now calling out and redeeming by His blood as they will appear glorified together with Him:

> "Then came one of the seven angels who had the seven bowls full of the seven last plagues and spoke to me, saying, 'Come, I will show you the Bride, the wife of the Lamb.' And he carried me away in the Spirit to a great, high mountain, and showed me the holy city Jerusalem coming down out of heaven from God, having the glory of God, its radiance like a most rare jewel, like a jasper, clear as crystal. It had a great, high wall, with twelve gates, and at the gates twelve angels, and on the gates the names of the twelve tribes of the sons of Israel were inscribed—on the east three gates, on the north three gates, on the south three gates, and on the west three gates. And the wall of the city had twelve foundations, and on them

were the twelve names of the twelve apostles of the Lamb.

And the one who spoke with me had a measuring rod of
gold to measure the city and its gates and walls. The city
lies foursquare, its length the same as its width. And he
measured the city with his rod, 12,000 stadia. Its length
and width and height are equal. He also measured its
wall, 144 cubits by human measurement, which is also an
angel's measurement. The wall was built of jasper, while
the city was pure gold, like clear glass. The foundations of
the wall of the city were adorned with every kind of jewel.
The first was jasper, the second sapphire, the third agate,
the fourth emerald, the fifth onyx, the sixth carnelian,
the seventh chrysolite, the eighth beryl, the ninth topaz,
the tenth chrysoprase, the eleventh jacinth, the twelfth
amethyst. And the twelve gates were twelve pearls, each of
the gates made of a single pearl, and the street of the city
was pure gold, like transparent glass.

And I saw no temple in the city, for its temple is the Lord
God the Almighty and the Lamb. And the city has no
need of sun or moon to shine on it, for the glory of God
gives it light, and its lamp is the Lamb. By its light will the
nations walk, and the kings of the earth will bring their
glory into it, and its gates will never be shut by day—and
there will be no night there. They will bring into it the
glory and the honor of the nations. But nothing unclean
will ever enter it, nor anyone who does what is detestable
or false, but only those who are written in the Lamb's
book of life. Then the angel showed me the river of the
water of life, bright as crystal, flowing from the throne of
God and of the Lamb through the middle of the street
of the city; also, on either side of the river, the tree of life
with its twelve kinds of fruit, yielding its fruit each month.
The leaves of the tree were for the healing of the nations.

No longer will there be anything accursed, but the throne of God and of the Lamb will be in it, and his servants will worship him. They will see his face, and his name will be on their foreheads. And night will be no more. They will need no light of lamp or sun, for the Lord God will be their light, and they will reign forever and ever" (Rev 21:9–22:5).

9

The Mystery of Iniquity

The term "kingdom of heaven" may rightfully be applied to any phase of the divine government in the earth. It has already passed through several distinct stages as recorded in history. God ruled through the patriarchs, judges and kings of Israel. The last rightful King of that nation was crowned with thorns. His rejection and crucifixion was the closing of the past dispensation and the grounds of blessing in the new age. Even before the cross His rejection was foreseen and the rejected King began from that time to speak of His death, the new dawning age, and of His return to this earth in power and glory. Then the rejected and postponed kingdom blessings were to be realized for Israel and all Gentile nations through them.

All this, even His rejection and the delay in the earthly kingdom, was in the foreknowledge and plan of God. Christ, as foreseen by prophets, was pictured in the figure of the coming "Lamb" sacrifice to be slain, as well as in the figure of the coming "Lion" King to reign; though the larger proportion of prophecy concerned itself with the latter. The prophets uttered these conflicting themes; they saw the sufferings and the glory; they did not comprehend the centuries of this church age that were to intervene. They saw the mountain peaks, but not the expanse of the valley of this age of grace. It pleased God to keep this period of time and its purpose as a sacred secret, or mystery, until the time of its realization. It is imperative that this fact should be understood, else an approach to Scriptural knowledge of the kingdom program is impossible.

Christ treated the present unannounced age as a sacred secret, or mystery, demanding explanation. Since His revelatory discussions on the subject it, like all other New Testament mysteries, remains no longer a mystery when explained. The preview of the facts of this mystery age are given in the seven parables of the thirteenth chapter of Matthew. It is also significant that this revelation of a new unforeseen age should follow immediately upon the first evidence of His rejection as Messiah King. These parables reveal the elements and conditions which characterize this age and which had been withheld in the councils of God. They are therefore spoken of as "the mysteries of the kingdom of heaven" (Matt 13:11), and this whole age may be rightfully termed "the kingdom of heaven in its mystery form." These parables treat of the beginning, course and end of the age which was then wholly future, but much of which has been faithfully fulfilled in the history of the Christian era.

The present period will therefore be seen to be that in which the kingdom of heaven in its mystery form is manifested and the divine unfolding of these mysteries to be a revelation of the present divine government and purposes in the earth. There are various other mysteries in the New Testament, some of which lend contributing elements to the one all-inclusive mystery age. Those New Testament mysteries which are related to the kingdom in its present form may be classified into three groups, each group representing a distinct purpose of God in the present age:

First, Israel's present position and age-long blindness is said to be a mystery:

> "Lest you be wise in your own sight, I do not want you to be unaware of this mystery, brothers: a partial hardening has come upon Israel, until the fullness of the Gentiles has come in. And in this way all Israel will be saved, as it is written, 'The Deliverer will come from Zion, he will banish ungodliness from Jacob'; 'and this will be my covenant with them when I take away their sins'" (Rom 11:25–27).

Second, the church is involved in four mysteries:

1. As the body now being formed out of both Jews and Gentiles

(Eph 3:1–10; Rom 16:25; Eph 6:19; Col 4:3).

2. As the bride of Christ (Eph 5:28–32).

3. As an organism by virtue of the indwelling Christ (Gal 2:20; Col 1:26, 27).

4. As to the manner of her departure from this earth (1 Cor 15:51–53; 1 Thess 4:13–18).

Third, the present age manifestation of the "mystery of lawlessness" (2 Thess 2:7; Matt 13:33; Rev 17:5, 7).

The central passage of this aspect of truth is here given:

> "Let no one deceive you in any way. For that day will not come, unless the rebellion comes first, and the man of lawlessness is revealed, the son of destruction, who opposes and exalts himself against every so-called god or object of worship, so that he takes his seat in the temple of God, proclaiming himself to be God. Do you not remember that when I was still with you I told you these things? And you know what is restraining him now so that he may be revealed in his time. For the mystery of lawlessness is already at work. Only he who now restrains it will do so until he is out of the way. And then the lawless one will be revealed, whom the Lord Jesus will kill with the breath of his mouth and bring to nothing by the appearance of his coming. The coming of the lawless one is by the activity of Satan with all power and false signs and wonders, and with all wicked deception for those who are perishing, because they refused to love the truth and so be saved" (2 Thess 2:3–10).

Paul, standing at the threshold of the new age, could say, "the mystery of lawlessness is already at work." He then declares that this will continue until its culmination in the "lawless one," the "man of lawlessness." This permitted development of the whole course of evil, he shows, will be under divine restraint in order that it may be consummated at the exact time divinely predetermined. Thus Israel's present blindness, the out-calling of the church and the final manifestations of evil will all be concluded in age-ending scenes; and these, taken together, form the distinguishing elements of the entire mystery age.

Iniquity had a definite beginning; it runs a well-defined course; it comes to a predicted end. It has been the evident purpose of God to put every assumption of Satan and fallen man to an experimental test. This was illustrated in the case of Job. God did not deny the challenge of Satan as to the faithfulness of Job; He rather gave Satan authority to make full trial. Another plan might have been easier for Job, but we must believe that enough was gained by the trial to warrant the plan. The experimental trial on the part of God of all issues flowing out of any challenge of the Creator on the part of the creature, explains, in part, the various testings of the ages. Much suffering and sorrow might have been averted had sin been wholly crushed at its beginning; but again we must believe that much more has been gained by the long delayed termination of evil. From the above passage it would seem that evil would have long concluded its own course in the lawlessness of fallen hearts had its natural energy not been restrained. It has been restrained, we are led to believe by the evidence, that the body and bride of Christ may be made complete.

The end of this age is outlined in an important body of Scripture which is found in portions of Old Testament prophecies, of the Gospels, and is a large portion of the writings of the second Epistles and Revelation. In all these records the disclosures concerning persons, times and events are in perfect agreement, though found in such widely separated sources, and to ignore them, or to form different conclusions than those which they predict, discredits the validity of the testimony of the one inspiring Spirit. The age is to end with a tribulation period which is not difficult to distinguish, chiefly from the fact that it is spoken of as the incomparable sorrow upon the earth:

"For then there will be great tribulation, such as has not
been from the beginning of the world until now, no, and
never will be. And if those days had not been cut short, no
human being would be saved. But for the sake of the elect
those days will be cut short" (Matt 24:21–22).

"At that time shall arise Michael, the great prince who
has charge of your people. And there shall be a time of
trouble, such as never has been since there was a nation till
that time. But at that time your people shall be delivered,
everyone whose name shall be found written in the book"
(Dan 12:1).

"A day of darkness and gloom, a day of clouds and thick
darkness! Like blackness there is spread upon the mountains a great and powerful people; their like has never been
before, nor will be again after them through the years of
all generations" (Joel 2:2).

"These are the words that the LORD spoke concerning
Israel and Judah: 'Thus says the LORD: We have heard
a cry of panic, of terror, and no peace. Ask now, and see,
can a man bear a child? Why then do I see every man with
his hands on his stomach like a woman in labor? Why has
every face turned pale? Alas! That day is so great there is
none like it; it is a time of distress for Jacob; yet he shall be
saved out of it" (Jer 30:4–7).

Three distinct divine purposes may be discovered in this tribulation
time. The passages here referred to are of great importance, but cannot
be quoted in full:

First, it is the time of "Jacob's trouble." Special and final judgments
upon the chosen people, which have long been foretold, will end their
age-long afflictions (Jer 25:29–38; 30:4–7; Ezek 30:3; Dan 12:1; Amos

5:18–20; Obad 1:15–21; Zeph 1:7–18; Zeph 12:1–14; 14:1–3; Malachi 4:1–4; Matt 24:9–31; Rev 7:13, 14).

Second, this period will be a time when judgment will fall on the Gentile nations and the sin of the whole earth (Job 21:30; Ps 2:5; Isa 2:10–22; 13:9–16; 24:21–23; 26:20, 21; 34:1–9; 63:1–6; 66:15–24; Jer 25:29–38; Ezek 30:3; Joel 3:9–21; Zeph 12:1–14; Matt 25:31–46; Rev 3:10; 11:1–18:24).

Third, this time is also characterized by the appearance and reign of the "man of lawlessness" whose career, like the period in which he appears, cannot begin until the divine restraint is removed (2 Thess 2:6–10), and will end with the return of Christ coming in power and great glory (2 Thess 2:8). This world-ruler is the fitting manifestation of the last efforts of Satan in his opposition against God and his attempted self-exaltation above the Most High.

Again, the church is nowhere seen nor in any way related to the tribulation period, which is constantly represented and distinctly said to be the time of "Jacob's trouble." There is great salvation during the tribulation and a mighty harvest of saints from it are seen in the glory, even a multitude which no man can number (Rev 7:9–17). It does not follow that these are a part of "the church which is his body" any more than that the saints of the Old Testament are a part of that body: rather the church is to be saved out of the hour of trial that shall come upon the earth to try all men (Rev 3:10).

Not only is this true in Old Testament types (judgment cannot fall on Sodom until Lot and his family are removed) but the tribulation is not once mentioned in the Epistles wherein the instruction and warnings are given to the church, nor does the church or the first resurrection appear in those passages which are descriptive of the tribulation. In the reckoning of God, most evidently, the tribulation, or time of Jacob's trouble, does not concern the church.

The character of the tribulation and its terrible display of the wrath of God is described in the successive judgments predicted in Revelation 2–19., but of the church it is said, "God has not destined us for wrath" (1 Thess 5:9; see also Rom 5:9; 1 Thess 1:10).

To contend that the church must pass through that unprecedented period virtually destroys every promise of His imminent return; for in such a case the church to be consistent must have her eyes on earth conditions when she is rather enjoined to be looking for her Lord from heaven. By such a theory the blessed hope is lost. So, also, the very martyrdom of loyal saints, in that period (Rev 13:15), would render groundless any hope for the translation of living saints at its end. And so, again, much that is most precious in church truth is confused and lost when related to "the time of Jacob's trouble."

As the Lord appears from heaven in power and great glory (Rev 19:11) He is accompanied by the armies of heaven, their identity being revealed by the white linen they wear (cf. Rev 19:14 with 7–10). At some previous time, the bride has met the Bridegroom, else how could she thus return with Him to reign? Is there not a danger in all this of saying, "My Lord delays his coming"?

The beginning, course and end of evil may be traced in four crises in the career of Satan. Sin began with him before recorded time when he said within the secret of his heart, "I will be like the Most High" (Isa 14:14). It began as an assumption against God and a purpose to be like Him as an independent being, to gain the worship of other beings, and the authority and government that belongs to God alone. Satan's sin appears again when he met the first man and woman in the garden. Here he pressed upon them the secret purpose of his own heart and the motive of his own action when he said, "be as gods." In the fall which has followed that choice we have a race wholly independent of God, assuming self-sufficiency, self-seeking and self-worship. The satanic principle of assumption toward God is therefore the present attitude of the fallen nature in its relation to God. Again, Satan met the last Adam in the wilderness. There was no occasion there for him to advise the Lord of Glory to assume to be God. Satan knew full well that He was Very God; yet his own heart's passion could not be restrained, for he said, "worship me." In the permissive providence of God, and under the evident experimental test of the mighty assumptions of Satan, the whole course of evil with its human governments and independence of God has developed. It was at work at the beginning of the age. It is to have its final manifestation and defeat at the end of the age. The last permitted demonstration of this timeless purpose of Satan will be by his masterpiece the world-ruling, world-worshipped "man of lawlessness" sitting in the restored temple and declaring himself to be very God (2 Thess 2:3–4). Christ warns those of His own nation who will be alive at the time of those terrible scenes that this "abomination of desolation," sitting in the holy place, is a sign of the end and that the testing of evil by Jehovah will then be consummated (Matt 24:15).

To Daniel was given the vision of the course and end of the entire Gentile world period extending from the last captivity until the setting up of the covenanted kingdom in the earth. He also sees the final form of iniquity as gathered up in the reign of the "Little Horn" (Dan 7:8, 20–26; 8:24, 25; 9:26, 27) and the willful king (Dan 11:36–45; 12:11). Ezekiel sees the same world-ruler as the "Prince of Tyre" (Ezek 28:1–10), and there closely related to Satan as the "King of Tyre" (Ezek 28:11–19). Christ speaks of him, quoting from Daniel, as the "Abomination of Desolation" (Matt 24:15; Dan 9:27), and, again, as the one who will come in his own name (John 5:43). John sees him as the rider on the white horse (Rev 6:2), and the "Beast" (Rev 13:4, 10). Paul sees him as the "man of lawlessness" (2 Thess 2:3).

In all these prophecies this coming one is set forth as being the superlative representation of Satan's power and the incarnate realization of his timeless secret purpose. Satan offered all his world power and authority to Christ in the wilderness (Luke 4:5–6), but it was rejected. This world power will be received and administered by the "man of lawlessness" during the closing scenes of the age.

It is not possible in the space allowed here, nor is it germane to the purpose of this book, to trace the details of revelation regarding the tribulation and the "man of lawlessness." This has been faithfully done by others and to some extent in the author's previous work, "Satan."

It may be concluded that the final demonstration of Satan's claim, with its certain failure, will prove him to have utterly failed in his ultimate aim, and then will every mouth be closed before the God of the whole earth. The righteous judgments of God against all wickedness, assumption and blasphemy will be accepted and His ways, which are past finding out, will be vindicated. "The mystery of lawlessness is already at work," but it must proceed to its determined end and this mighty development of evil is one of the divine purposes of the entire period of this mystery age. God incarnate in the Son is a New Testament mystery (1 Tim 3:16), and Satan, seeking to be as God, and incarnate in the "man of lawlessness" will, in that being, execute the final manifestation of the age-long "mystery of lawlessness."

10

The Mysteries of the Kingdom of Heaven

Unto Daniel, a prophet of the exile, was given the vision of the course of the whole Gentile period extending from the last captivity to the second coming of Christ—that period spoken of in Scripture as "the time of the Gentiles" (Luke 21:24). Daniel forecasts the movements of the successive Gentile world powers during this period. He first interprets King Nebuchadnezzar's dream (2:37–45) as descriptive of four successive world powers. The same is again revealed in Daniel's dream (7:1–28) by the vision of four beasts, and again in the dream as recorded in the eighth chapter. By all these revelations the Gentile world governments then in view and which are to occupy the power and authority during the "times of the Gentiles," are seen to be Babylonia, Medo-Persia, Greece and Rome. The latter of these is seen to be divided and subdivided as are the legs and toes of the great image, thus anticipating the present division of that territory as gathered about the two centers, Constantinople and Rome and the final ten governments yet to hold sway simultaneously on the original Roman empire.

Daniel also sees the same period as continuing seventy weeks of years, or heptads (Dan 9:24–27). In this vision this Gentile time of seventy heptads is divided into two distinct periods. One, the time before the "cutting off" of Messiah, in other words, the rejection of Christ; and the other, the time after that event. Sixty-nine weeks, or heptads, were required for the fulfillment of the first period. This began with

Daniel's time, or when the edict to restore Jerusalem was sent forth, and ended with the cutting off of Messiah. This was exactly fulfilled in the 483 years (69 x 7) before Christ. As the prophets in their foreview evidently took no account of time during which Israel was to be cut off from national blessings, the present church age, which began with the cross of Christ and ends at an unrevealed time, is in no instance considered in their foreview, and the remaining moments of the prophesied time will not be counted off until this mystery age of the church has been completed.

The remaining predicted period, the seventieth week, or heptad, which is the time of the great tribulation (Dan 9:27) has yet to run its course to complete the whole time required to "to finish the transgression, to put an end to sin, and to atone for iniquity, to bring in everlasting righteousness, to seal both vision and prophet, and to anoint a most holy place." Thus it would seem clear that a period of seven years (shortened a little, Matt 24:22) will follow the present unpredicted period of the out-calling of the church and precede the setting up of Messiah's kingdom. Notwithstanding the fact that the mystery age of the church did not come into the prophet's view, the time of the final heptad, or period of seven, was seen to be much delayed; for it was given to him to understand "what is to happen to your people in the latter days."

Daniel sees the entire period of the "times of the Gentiles" extending from the captivity, through 483 years to the cross, and on beyond to the dateless coming of the "Ancient of Days" and the setting up of a kingdom by the God of Heaven which shall never be destroyed. "It shall break in pieces all these kingdoms and bring them to an end, and it shall stand forever" (Dan 2:44, 45; 7:13, 14).

The portion of "the times of the Gentiles" following the cross, including as it does the church age, is clearly indefinite aside from the events assigned to Daniel's last "week" (cf. Dan 9:26 with Matt 24:6–14). This, as might be expected, is the divine method of accurately forecasting Israel's future while reserving any clear light on the sacred secret of this mystery age. There was no secret regarding the "times of the Gentiles," with the attending present position of Israel in the world; but hidden within that era is a briefer period, "the fullness of the Gentiles" (Rom 11:25) about which nothing had been revealed. It is the church that is the "fullness of him who fills all in all," and that body completed is the "measure of the stature of the fullness of Christ" (Eph 1:23; 4:13; Acts 15:13–14; 1 Cor 12:12–13). It is clear, therefore, that a mystery age has been thrust, as a parenthesis, into that which had been previously revealed for the fulfillment of the purpose of God.

The moral character of this mystery age at its beginning, like its moral development and end are clearly presented in the New Testament. At the very beginning the inspired writers spoke of it as an evil age:

> "Who gave himself for our sins to deliver us from the present evil age" (Gal 1:4).

> "Do not be conformed to this world [age]" (Rom 12:2).

> "For Demas, in love with this present world [age], has deserted me" (2 Tim 4:10).

> "In their case the god of this world [age] has blinded the minds of the unbelievers" (2 Cor 4:4).

So the church was fully warned from the beginning as to this age, and taught concerning her pilgrim character while here and her holy calling and separateness from the "evil age." A portion of the time during which Israel was to be dispersed and deprived of national blessing had been divinely accounted for by the "seventy weeks" revelation given to Daniel. The fact and purpose of this present mystery age was not mentioned in this revelation; hence there was need that this sacred secret should be revealed when its time had fully come. This Jesus does in the seven parables of Matthew 13, it being ever God's method to give a foreview of all His great purposes and undertakings. The course and moral development of this age is here divinely presented in these parables and this, together with Daniel's seventy weeks, completes the revelation with respect to the entire period known as "the times of the Gentiles."

In these parables this parenthetical age covering the timeless period between Daniel's sixty-ninth and seventieth weeks is treated as the mystery form of the kingdom of heaven. It is the government of God over a period of various mystery purposes in the earth, to wit; the continued blindness of Israel throughout the age, the consummation, at the end, of all forms of evil, and the out-calling of the church.

Each of the age-characterizing mysteries is said to be terminated by the same event. The blindness of Israel, mentioned in Romans 11:25, is followed by the promise: "And in this way all Israel will be saved, as it is written, 'The Deliverer will come from Zion, he will banish ungodliness from Jacob'; 'and this will be my covenant with them when I take away their sins" (Rom 11:26–27). So the career of the "man of lawlessness," who is said to be the consummation of the "mystery of lawlessness," is ended thus: "whom the Lord Jesus will kill with the breath of his mouth and bring to nothing by the appearance of his coming" (2 Thess 2:8). So, also, it is written concerning the completion of the calling out of the church: "After this I will return" (Acts 15:13–16). These great sacred secrets, it will be noticed, constitute the very elements in the parables which define the character and object of the age.

In the first of the parables a sower goes forth to sow; but only a fourth part of the seed thus sown comes to full development. The parable is interpreted by Christ and so permits of no speculation:

"Hear then the parable of the sower: When anyone hears the word of the kingdom and does not understand it, the evil one comes and snatches away what has been sown in his heart. This is what was sown along the path. As for what was sown on rocky ground, this is the one who hears the word and immediately receives it with joy, yet he has no root in himself, but endures for a while, and when tribulation or persecution arises on account of the word, immediately he falls away. As for what was sown among thorns, this is the one who hears the word, but the cares of the world and the deceitfulness of riches choke the word, and it proves unfruitful. As for what was sown on good soil, this is the one who hears the word and understands

it. He indeed bears fruit and yields, in one case a hun-
dredfold, in another sixty, and in another thirty" (Matt
13:18–23).

In full agreement with experience during the past nineteen hundred
years of Christian history the parable teaches that a great portion of those
to whom the Word is preached are not saved by it, and lest it might
be concluded by His hearers that, while this was the condition at the
beginning of the age it would not be so at the end, the second parable,
that of the wheat and the tares, immediately follows. This, like the first,
is interpreted by Christ Himself and its meaning is made plain:

> "The one who sows the good seed is the Son of Man.
> The field is the world, and the good seed is the sons of
> the kingdom. The weeds are the sons of the evil one, and
> the enemy who sowed them is the devil. The harvest is
> the end of the age, and the reapers are angels. Just as the
> weeds are gathered and burned with fire, so will it be at the
> end of the age. The Son of Man will send his angels, and
> they will gather out of his kingdom all causes of sin and
> all law-breakers, and throw them into the fiery furnace.
> In that place there will be weeping and gnashing of teeth.
> Then the righteous will shine like the sun in the kingdom
> of their Father. He who has ears, let him hear" (Matt
> 13:37–43).

In this parable the born-again ones, the members of His body, are seen
as the "wheat," or the "children of God" amidst the whole sphere of
religious profession and assumption. It is important to note the age-closing scenes according to this interpretation: "So will it be at the end of
the age." Certainly this does not depict a regenerated world. It clearly
pictures an out-called people together with the full ripening of iniquity
in the unregenerate portion of humanity.

The third parable is not interpreted, nor is any following it explained; but enough has been revealed by the two interpretations to form a key to all that follow. They present aspects of the kingdom of heaven in the one mystery form and so must be in fullest agreement. In the third parable He presents truth through the figure of the mustard seed and tree. Again the testimony of history and the teaching of the parable agree. The very small beginning in the early days of the church has developed out of all due proportion in mere members and includes all professing Christendom. The great tree now shelters even the birds of the air. It is significant that the birds of the first parable are represented as catching away the good seed. The truly saved ones are still a "little flock" compared with the multitude of nominal church supporters.

The fourth parable is of the three measures of meal which all became leavened. Throughout the Bible leaven symbolizes evil, and Jesus fully defined His use of the word on other occasions. He used the word to represent evil doctrine to the extent of formality (Matt 23:14, 16, 23–28), unbelief (Matt 22:23, 29; Mark 8:15), and worldliness (Matt 22:16–21; Mark 3:6). Paul uses the same word with reference to "malice and evil" (1 Cor 5:6–8). Its process of working is by a subtle permeating of the mass into which it is introduced. This much misunderstood parable teaches, in accord with the other parables and all related Scripture, that which has proven to be consonant with experience in the history of the age, namely, that even the true believers, and certainly the mass of professors, will be sadly influenced by these various forms of evil. There can be no question but that this has been true to the present hour.

The fifth parable is evidently a teaching concerning Israel, His "treasure" (Exod 19:5; Deut 4:20), including all the tribes, hid in the field, which is the world. When He shall call forth His "treasure" it will be by virtue of the fact that He hath, as the Lamb of God, taken away the sins of the world. One, we are told, sold all and purchased that field. What Jehovah may do now, or at any time in behalf of any people, will be because of the atoning value of the priceless blood of His Son. The Only Begotten Son was given for the world.

The mystery of the church, the pearl of great cost, as set forth in the sixth parable, has already been considered. She is not now hid in the field, the world; but is being formed there, and is awaiting her coming glory when, in the ages to come, she shall display His glory and grace. She too is redeemed at the same priceless cost (1 Pet 1:18).

The last parable restates the fact of the outworking of the two great mysteries—the out-called church and the mystery of iniquity, as co-existing to the time of the end. The good fish shall be gathered into vessels and the bad shall be cast away. "So will it be at the end of the age." Thus the three great mysteries of this mystery age were related in the teachings of Jesus to the beginning course and end of the present age.

The following Scriptures give added light on the thought and expectation of Christ and the apostles concerning the course and end of this age:

> "And Jesus answered them, 'See that no one leads you astray. For many will come in my name, saying, 'I am the Christ,' and they will lead many astray. And you will hear of wars and rumors of wars. See that you are not alarmed, for this must take place, but the end is not yet. For nation will rise against nation, and kingdom against kingdom, and there will be famines and earthquakes in various places. All these are but the beginning of the birth pains'" (Matt 24:4–8).

> "For as were the days of Noah, so will be the coming of the Son of Man" (Matt 24:37).

> "I have become all things to all people, that by all means I might save some" (1 Cor 9:22).

> "Now the Spirit expressly says that in later times some will depart from the faith by devoting themselves to deceitful spirits and teachings of demons" (1 Tim 4:1).

> "But understand this, that in the last days there will come

times of difficulty" (2 Tim 3:1).

"While evil people and impostors will go on from bad to worse, deceiving and being deceived" (2 Tim 3:13).

"For the time is coming when people will not endure sound teaching, but having itching ears they will accumulate for themselves teachers to suit their own passions, and will turn away from listening to the truth and wander off into myths" (2 Tim 4:3–4).

"Knowing this first of all, that scoffers will come in the last days with scoffing, following their own sinful desires. They will say, "Where is the promise of his coming? For ever since the fathers fell asleep, all things are continuing as they were from the beginning of creation" (2 Pet 3:3–4).

To this may be added the other parables of Jesus regarding the kingdom in its mystery form and the whole divinely given history of the church as previewed in Revelation 2:1–3:22. So, also, the more detailed description of the age-ending scenes as given by Daniel and in Revelation 4:1–20:3.

There is an age of universal blessing coming upon the earth; but it is in no way represented in Scripture to be any part, or product, of this mystery age. On the other hand, it is revealed that it will be ushered in by the same divine movements that form the closing scenes of this age. The impelling motive of the service of saints at the present time must be nothing less than the world-wide testimony to the Gospel of God's grace through which Christ may finish the gathering out of a people for His Person and soon complete His bride. The great soul-winners of past generations have been actuated by this vision and purpose, and there could hardly be a ministry in the mind and power of the Spirit that did not wholly agree with the revealed purpose of God in the present mystery age.

11

The Call of the Bridegroom

Immediately before His death Jesus delivered two great discourses which served to culminate His teaching ministry. Though spoken at about the same time and to the same disciples there is the widest difference between them. One, "The Olivet discourse" (Matt 24:4–25:46, and Luke 21:20–24), was spoken from the very Mount of Olives where His feet shall stand when He returns to the earth (Zech 14:4). In this discourse only His own nation Israel is in view, and His instruction to them is of the events leading up to, and accompanying, His coming to the world in mighty judgments as King of kings and Lord of lords, and of the establishment, at that time, of the long delayed earthly kingdom. These great events had been before the eyes of prophets and seers from Moses to Christ, and will fulfill all covenants and promises for Israel including a world-wide Gentile blessing through them. This discourse naturally appears in the Gospel of the King, and completes the testimony committed to Matthew.

The other closing discourse was given in the upper room and continued on the way to the garden (John 13:1–17:26). The subjects He presents to the disciples are those blessings that flow out of His death and resurrection; for here He speaks as though His cross was an accomplished fact. Thus the disciples are not now addressed as of the nation Israel; but as of the heavenly company who, by that cross, have come into heavenly union with Him (John 14:20). Matthew records that John the Baptist announced Jesus as King: John records that he announced Jesus as "The Lamb of God who takes away the sin of the world." Matthew has a nation in view, with its covenanted earthly kingdom: John has the individual in view, with the heavenly glory of the bride of Christ. In Matthew's Gospel the coming judgments and sorrows of earth with the following earthly glory are in view. In John's presentation the sacrificial atoning judgments of the cross and the heavenly glory are in view. In the one, the return of the King to the earth is presented: in the other, the call of the Bridegroom when He shall receive His bride from the earth into the mansion He has gone to prepare is recorded. One discourse is addressed to and concerns Israel in the earth: the other is addressed to and concerns the born-again ones of all nations who, by His grace, are already citizens of heaven. Each writer draws from the doings and teachings of Christ the particular materials required to present the picture divinely assigned to him.

No event, unless it be the cross, is more emphasized in Scripture than the personal return of Christ to this earth. This truth occupies at least one verse in twenty of the New Testament, and is not only the subject of the last words of Jesus to His own in the world, but is the subject of the closing words and promise of the Bible itself. John, who had been with Jesus on earth and in the glory, who had heard His promise to return again and who, in the Spirit, had witnessed those representations of the age-closing scenes as recorded in the Revelation, could say in answer to that final promise of Christ: "Amen. Even so, come, Lord Jesus." John certainly had all the facts before him, and if any child of God does not find the same response in his heart to the last promise of Jesus would it not be well to discover the unhappy cause?

The general fact of a return of Christ has, of necessity, found its way into all evangelical creeds; but individual readers who have hesitated to believe the literal promises of unfulfilled prophecy, have invented numerous interpretations of this body of Scripture. As must follow, every false interpretation utterly fails, at some point or points, to adequately deal with all the facts of revelation. If Christ's promised return was fulfilled at Pentecost by the coming of the Spirit, then the two Persons of the Godhead are confused and every New Testament writer is found to be a false witness in that they each, writing long after Pentecost, presented the return of Christ as a then future event. If His return is said to be fulfilled in the death of a believer, because of the fact that he then goes to be with

Christ, there is a sad ignoring of every predicted event accompanying that return and a hopeless confusion of what the Scriptures call the "last enemy" and "the blessed hope." If His return is represented as fulfilled by the results of evangelization, on the ground that Christ is said to come into the life of every saved one, then a process has been substituted for that which in Scripture is said to be visible, sudden and personal, and every recorded circumstance and event accompanying His return has been ignored or forgotten. If He is to return only after a millennium of a saved and sanctified earth, ushered in by the present form of Christian ministry and service, the numerous injunctions to be personally "watching," "waiting," "looking" and "loving" could well be taken as irony in the light of the fact that even a tendency toward such a man-made millennium is not discernible after two thousand years of God's dealings in grace with the children of men. If Satan, "released for a little while" (Rev 20:3), can utterly spoil a full ripened millennium, what human agency can hope to establish that millennium while Satan still usurps the throne of this world (2 Cor 4:3–4)? Scripture plainly predicts the sudden and violent imprisonment of that mighty age-ruler by the power of the returning Christ before any universal kingdom blessings can be secured on the earth (Rev 19:11–20:3; 2 Thess 2:1–10). It is not at all a question of whether the Holy Spirit, now present in the world, could bind Satan and set up a kingdom in the earth, nor is it belittling to the work of the Spirit to point out that this is not the revealed purpose: rather, the whole question turns, and turns only, on what the revealed purpose of God is, which purpose must be determined in the light of every promise and event contained in the whole body of Scripture. A system of interpretation which does not account for every detail of revelation fails, in so far as it does not so account, to expose the meaning of the Word of God. If the same liberty were taken in the interpretation of redemptive truth that is often taken in prophetic truth, the doors would be instantly flung open to every soul-destroying heresy of the present time.

The thoughtful reader of Scripture has observed that the passages usually supposed to relate to the return of Christ naturally gather into two classes, or groups, totally different as to time, purpose and events.

In one class of passages it is not represented that Christ will appear on the earth, or to any but His own redeemed people. These passages affirm that at this appearing the bodies of sleeping saints will come forth from the graves and, together with saints living on the earth, are to be caught up to meet Him in the air and thus are to be forever with the Lord. In the other class of passages, His return is to the earth, visibly, suddenly, in power and great glory, accompanied with the national judgments and followed by the setting up of His kingdom in the earth. In this group of prophecies the Lord is seen to bring a mighty army of redeemed with Him and they are to share with Him His kingly reign.

Very much must yet be fulfilled, according to Scripture, before the events connected with the visible return of Christ to the earth are to occur (2 Thess 2:1–10). In contradistinction, however, no prophecy remains unfulfilled which in its order precedes the coming into the air to call for His own (1 Thess 4:13–18), other than that the outgathered bride shall have made herself ready; and, therefore, that coming to call His own is the next event in the prophetic program. Of that day and hour no man could know; but all generations of saints have been instructed to "watch," "wait," "look," "love" and "be ready." These words are descriptive of the attitude of heart of a bride awaiting the return of the one on whom all her life and love is centered. Especially would this be true if she knew not the day nor hour when he would return.

This call of the Bridegroom for His bride is an event that should never have been considered even as an aspect of the second coming of Christ. It is a mystery, or sacred secret, and, as such, is but a part of the whole mystery of the body and bride of Christ. It is only one Item in the program of the out-calling and final gathering of the church. No revelation had been given to the Old Testament prophets of that great age purpose, and certainly no hint had been made as to the manner in which she would be taken out of the earth into her heavenly bliss. On the other hand, the return of Christ to the earth in power and glory was seen by all the prophets from Moses to Christ. They beheld it as the consummation of all earthly blessings. The one, revealed only when the time for explaining the mystery was ripe, concerns a redeemed and heavenly people as to the manner of their final departure from this world:

the other, foreseen by all the prophets, concerns Israel and the nations as to their judgments and final positions in a kingdom on the earth. Of the first event it is written:

> "Behold! I tell you a mystery. We shall not all sleep, but we shall all be changed, in a moment, in the twinkling of an eye, at the last trumpet. For the trumpet will sound, and the dead will be raised imperishable, and we shall be changed" (1 Cor 15:51–52).

This mystery, that not all should die, but that some should be changed "in a moment, in the twinkling of an eye, at the last trumpet," was never before revealed. So again in 1 Thessalonians 4:13–18:

> "But we do not want you to be uninformed, brothers, about those who are asleep, that you may not grieve as others do who have no hope. For since we believe that Jesus died and rose again, even so, through Jesus, God will bring with him those who have fallen asleep. For this we declare to you by a word from the Lord, that we who are alive, who are left until the coming of the Lord, will not precede those who have fallen asleep. For the Lord himself will descend from heaven with a cry of command, with the voice of an archangel, and with the sound of the trumpet of God. And the dead in Christ will rise first. Then we who are alive, who are left, will be caught up together with them in the clouds to meet the Lord in the air, and so we will always be with the Lord. Therefore encourage one another with these words."

The dead in Christ will be raised first and the living saints caught up, and together they shall all go on in clouds to meet the Lord in the air (see Gen 5:24; 2 Kgs 2:11) and to be forever with the Lord.

In the two passages quoted above, Paul, by the use of the pronoun "we," has five times included himself as possibly to be among the living ones at the time of the Lord's call for His bride. This precludes a doubt as to the belief of the great Apostle in the imminent, personal, premillennial return of Christ. This hope was evidently his greatest motive for true character and service. So it has been to the great missionaries and soul winners since his day.

A great moral effect was divinely intended in the promise of the imminent appearing of Christ. The church that has lost hope to the extent that she could say, "My Lord delays his coming," has soon been drunk with the wine of this world. It was this blessed expectation that was intended to teach us "to renounce ungodliness and worldly passions, and to live self-controlled, upright, and godly lives in the present age, waiting for our blessed hope, the appearing of the glory of our great God and Savior Jesus Christ" (Titus 2:12–13).

Only an apostate age could doubt this promise, Peter tells us:

> "Knowing this first of all, that scoffers will come in the
> last days with scoffing, following their own sinful desires.
> They will say, 'Where is the promise of his coming? For
> ever since the fathers fell asleep, all things are continuing as
> they were from the beginning of creation'" (2 Pet 3:3–4).

The eternal blessings of seeing His face and the reunion with loved ones gone before are by this hope but a moment removed. It is therefore the "blessed hope" and the comforting hope. We did not turn to God from idols to serve the living and true God and to wait for death; but rather to "wait for his Son from heaven" (1 Thess 1:9–10). How natural for one who has really come to love Him to also "love his appearing" (2 Tim 4:8) above all the things of earth. The sweetest experiences foreshadowed in the bridal unions of the Old Testament and those experiences which are anticipated in the New Testament await that unannounced, signless and timeless summons to be forever at rest in His bosom of love:

"Let not your hearts be troubled. Believe in God; believe
also in me. In my Father's house are many rooms. If it were
not so, would I have told you that I go to prepare a place
for you? And if I go and prepare a place for you, I will
come again and will take you to myself, that where I am
you may be also (John 14:1–3).

I know not when the Lord will come,
Or at what hour He may appear.
Whether at midnight, or at morn,
Or at what season of the year.
I only know that He is near,
And that His voice I soon shall hear.

If the pastor is mourning over the cold, unspiritual condition of his
church, let him consider the warm, glowing love and devoted service
that has always accompanied the right understanding of this "blessed
hope." If the church is given to carelessness and worldliness, let him
recall that for this there has been provided the "purifying hope." As
under-shepherds shall we not go down on our faces before God and there
question whether we have been giving these dependent ones their "food
in due season"?

12

The Olivet Discourse

It has pleased the Spirit to present in the Gospel by Matthew the final revelations of the kingdom. These begin with the birth of the King, follow through His rejection, picture the mystery form of the kingdom, and predict the return of the King to the earth, the sphere of the kingdom of heaven. Like the Old

Testament prophets, this kingdom traces only the movements of Israel, her failures, her sorrows, and her coming blessings under the reign of her returning Messiah King. In this Gospel the church appears incidentally as one of the several mysteries of a mystery age. In this body of Scripture the walk and destiny of the church are not once in view.

The events leading up to the realization of the kingdom in the earth are given by Matthew in their exact order. He begins with the lineage and birth of the King. This is followed by the announcement by the King, by John the Baptist and by the disciples, of the kingdom as at hand, with a call for the great predicted national repentance. During this season of the offered kingdom, the King announces the principles of righteousness that must obtain when the kingdom comes. He teaches them to pray: "Your kingdom come, your will be done, on earth as it is in heaven." The eleventh chapter records the first evidence of the rejection of the King—the imprisonment of His forerunner. From this time the Jews take counsel to kill the King and the national rejection of His kingly claims is seen to deepen, as He faithfully continues to offer Himself, until their final answer to that offer is His crucifixion by the rulers of the nation. Yet even after His ascension, the unmeasured grace of God is seen in the final renewal of the kingdom offer to that nation through the Apostle Peter in his second sermon in Jerusalem. Peter begins by declaring that God's covenants will all be fulfilled, and that the death of Christ was anticipated by the prophets, and is now accomplished. He presents Christ as having been received into heaven to remain until the restitution of all things spoken of by the prophets. This is not a Gentile church enlarged to encompass the earth; but the mighty restoration of the Davidic order and the everlasting reestablishment of the chosen nation in their own land, in full kingdom blessing, all of which God has sworn with an oath to perform. This final appeal, like those which preceded it, was made with the same repentance in view: "Repent, that the times of refreshing may come from the presence of the Lord." The answer of the nation to this appeal was the imprisonment of the messengers and the placing of the official ban upon their message.

As the evidence of rejection began to appear, according to Matthew, Jesus began to speak of His decease, of the hitherto unannounced mystery age, and that to be followed by His return to the earth as King in world-transforming scenes of judgment and the final establishment of the kingdom in the earth. Yet it must be remembered that only Israel is addressed and in this Gospel nations are seen only as related to her. Thus this Gospel is presented true to the exact scope of the kingdom of heaven.

Preceding the "Olivet discourse" of Matthew 24:4–25:46 a picture is given of the love of Christ for His nation and Jerusalem, the city of the great King.

> "O Jerusalem, Jerusalem, the city that kills the prophets and stones those who are sent to it! How often would I have gathered your children together as a hen gathers her brood under her wings, and you were not willing! See, your house is left to you desolate. For I tell you, you will not see me again, until you say, 'Blessed is he who comes in the name of the Lord'" (Matt 23:37–39).

He would oft have gathered them (as He will yet do according to Matt 24:31); but they would not.

Their house is left unto them desolate; but not forever. "You will not see me again, until you say, 'Blessed is he who comes in the name of the Lord.'"

The "Olivet discourse," it should be noted, was the Lord's reply to three questions asked of him by His disciples:

First, "When will these things be?" referring to His preceding prophecy as to the levelling of the stones of the temple to the ground. This first question is not answered in Matthew's account, but is found in Luke 21:20–24:

> "But when you see Jerusalem surrounded by armies, then know that its desolation has come near. Then let those who are in Judea flee to the mountains, and let those who are inside the city depart, and let not those who are out in the country enter it, for these are days of vengeance, to fulfill all that is written. Alas for women who are pregnant and for those who are nursing infants in those days! For there will be great distress upon the earth and wrath against this people. They will fall by the edge of the sword and be led captive among all nations, and Jerusalem will be trampled underfoot by the Gentiles, until the times of the Gentiles are fulfilled."

This catastrophe, we are told, occurred in the year 70 AD.

The second question: "What will be the sign of your coming?" and the third: "and of the end of the age?" are answered in Matthew's account beginning with 24:4.

In opening this discourse Christ first describes the character of the whole age leading up to His return in power and great glory (24:30). The emphasis here is wholly on the end-time and its character, according to the request of His disciples. He, however, forecasts the whole time from the hour He was speaking through to the end. He divides this time into two periods. The first of these, extending over nearly the whole period, or up to the last seven years, is characterized by war, famine, pestilence and earthquake which are doubtless to become increasingly violent as the time of the end draws near. He distinctly states that these age-long characteristics are common to the whole age, rather than constituting the end, or a sign of the end. The passage is as follows:

> "And Jesus answered them, 'See that no one leads you astray. For many will come in my name, saying, 'I am the Christ,' and they will lead many astray. And you will hear of wars and rumors of wars. See that you are not alarmed, for this must take place, but the end is not yet. For nation will rise against nation, and kingdom against kingdom, and there will be famines and earthquakes in various places. All these are but the beginning of the birth pains'" (Matt 24:4–8).

This prophecy of the character of the age has been proven by nearly two thousand years of history. It is now seen to be as accurate a description of the age as a present-day historian, looking back over the centuries, could write. In spite of the dreams of peace for the "great enlightened twentieth century," so fresh in our minds, it stands without a parallel, even in its fifteenth year, as the superlative in all that the Lord Himself assigned as characterizing features of this age. These positive predictions, among many others, which find no possible Biblical interpretation against them, fell from the lips of the Son of God and have been verified by the terrible facts of history up to the present hour; yet men dream of peace by manmade treaties and agreements as though our God had never spoken, or centuries of human greed and cruelty had not been experienced. War plainly belongs to the kingdom of Satan. It will cease for a thousand years while he is in the pit; but it will be instantly revived with all its horrors as soon as he is released for a little while (Rev 20:1–9). Jesus said to Pilate: "My kingdom is not of this world. If my kingdom were of this world, my servants would have been fighting" (John 18:36). War results from the fallen nature of man, and is under the power of Satan, and will be until that mighty being is chained and put in the pit and the world-transforming kingdom of Messiah is set up in the earth. "To the end there shall be war. Desolations are decreed" (Dan 9:26).

The war, famine, pestilence and earthquake features, which characterize this entire age, were spoken of by Christ as "the beginning of the birth pains" (Matt 24:8). This evidently anticipates a time of sorrow, or of birth. He then proceeds to describe this coming period as the "great tribulation," which, as has been seen, is no other than the long-predicted "time of Jacob's trouble," the time for the consummation of the "mystery of lawlessness" and the final judgments on the whole Gentile world, to be terminated, as set forth in all other passages on the subject, by the resistless power and glory of the coming King.

The description of this sorrow, or tribulation time, begins with the ninth verse. The time word "then," with which this verse opens, serves to shift the scenes from what has characterized the age to those conditions which will *"then"* prevail: "*Then* they will deliver you up to tribulation and put you to death, and you will be hated by all nations for my name's sake" (Matt 24:9). This was distinctly addressed to Jews; for they alone could be "hated of all nations." It is the "time of Jacob's trouble" and they are the "elect" mentioned throughout the passage. He then said:

> "And then many will fall away and betray one another
> and hate one another. And many false prophets will arise
> and lead many astray. And because lawlessness will be
> increased, the love of many will grow cold. But the one
> who endures to the end will be saved" (Matt 24:10–13).

This is not a condition of final salvation under grace: it was addressed to a nation who were to experience great tribulation, and forms a promise that will be most precious to those to whom it shall apply. So, also, the verse that follows is often confused with the present gospel of grace: "And this gospel of the kingdom will be proclaimed throughout the whole world as a testimony to all nations, and then the end will come" (Matt 24:14). A call to national repentance and the final announcement of the kingdom must yet again be taken up, as it will be by 144,000 sealed

ones, and by the two witnesses, before the King returns (Rev 7:4–11:19).
There is no such geographical demand on the preaching of grace in this
age: on the contrary, the preaching here referred to cannot begin until
the preaching of grace has accomplished its end in the calling out of His
bride, which event and people are not at all in view in this great discourse.
His bride will have been taken to Himself (before Matt 24:9), for she
is to be kept from the hour of trial that shall come on all the world to
try them that dwell upon the earth (Rev 3:10). There will doubtless be
great numbers saved during the tribulation (Rev 7:12–17). They will
not, however, have part in the special blessings of the bride; for when she
shall have entered in, the door will be shut.

Jesus then anticipates the "man of lawlessness" standing in the "holy
place" as foreseen by Daniel and later more fully described by Paul
(2 Thess 2:1–9), and John (Rev 13:3–10). This is followed by special
warnings which are very similar to those given to the same nation with
regard to the destruction of Jerusalem which took place in 70 AD. The
conditions of siege and the tribulation will be so similar that the warnings
are almost identical; but it does not follow that they anticipate the same
event. One is but a foreshadow of the other. The passage reads thus:

> "So when you see the abomination of desolation spoken
> of by the prophet Daniel, standing in the holy place (let
> the reader understand), then let those who are in Judea
> flee to the mountains. Let the one who is on the housetop
> not go down to take what is in his house, and let the one
> who is in the field not turn back to take his cloak. And
> alas for women who are pregnant and for those who are
> nursing infants in those days! Pray that your flight may
> not be in winter or on a Sabbath. For then there will be
> great tribulation, such as has not been from the beginning
> of the world until now, no, and never will be. And if
> those days had not been cut short, no human being would
> be saved. But for the sake of the elect those days will be
> cut short. Then if anyone says to you, 'Look, here is the

Christ!' or 'There he is!' do not believe it. For false christs
and false prophets will arise and perform great signs and
wonders, so as to lead astray, if possible, even the elect. See,
I have told you beforehand. So, if they say to you, 'Look,
he is in the wilderness,' do not go out. If they say, 'Look,
he is in the inner rooms,' do not believe it. For as the
lightning comes from the east and shines as far as the west,
so will be the coming of the Son of Man. Wherever the
corpse is, there the vultures will gather. Immediately after
the tribulation of those days the sun will be darkened,
and the moon will not give its light, and the stars will
fall from heaven, and the powers of the heavens will be
shaken. Then will appear in heaven the sign of the Son
of Man, and then all the tribes of the earth will mourn,
and they will see the Son of Man coming on the clouds of
heaven with power and great glory. And he will send out
his angels with a loud trumpet call, and they will gather
his elect from the four winds, from one end of heaven to
the other" (Matt 24:15–31).

In this passage it is important to note that the coming of Christ in
power and great glory is the termination of the tribulation and time of
Israel's regathering, as has been predicted by the prophets from Moses to
Christ. The same order obtains in all similar passages (see Acts 15:13–18;
2 Thess 2:1–10; so of the prophets and the Revelation). Israel, as a nation, not one generation, is to be divinely preserved until all be fulfilled:

> "Truly, I say to you, this generation will not pass away
> until all these things take place. Heaven and earth will pass
> away, but my words will not pass away" (Matt 24:34–35).

The returning Christ will find it on the earth as it was in the days of
Noah (24:38), when some shall be taken away in judgment and some
left for kingdom blessing. This is the opposite of the calling away of the

bride, then some are taken for blessing and some are left in judgment and sorrow. The return of Christ is then presented as a testing of all profession under the parable of the ten virgins, and the test of all service under the parable of the talents. So, also, "When the Son of Man comes in his glory, and all the angels with him, then he will sit on his glorious throne. Before him will be gathered all the nations, and he will separate people one from another as a shepherd separates the sheep from the goats" (25:31–32).

This is in no way comparable with the Great White Throne judgment of Revelation 20:11–15. That is at the end of a thousand years of kingdom blessing: this is before. All is different in time, place and subjects, as well as conditions. This judgment is of nations at the end of the time of Jacob's trouble and concerns their treatment of "my brethren" according to the flesh. The issue is to those on His right hand: "Come, you who are blessed by my Father, inherit the kingdom prepared for you from the foundation of the world" (Matt 25:34).

13

The Return of The King

Those passages which describe the calling of the bride to meet the Bridegroom in the air are enriched with words of certainty and assurance. It is as though that event which had not been made known until the present age, and which portends such immediate blessings for the child of God should need a special emphasis upon its certainty to strengthen the feeble faith of those to whom it is addressed. "If it were not so, I would have told you." "This we declare to you by a word from the Lord." "This Jesus, who was taken up from you into heaven, will come in the same way as you saw him go into heaven." Paul, when praying that we might know what is the hope of His calling and what the riches of the glory of His inheritance in the saints, adds the word of assurance that this will all be accomplished "according to the working of his great might that he worked in Christ when he raised him from the dead and seated him at his right hand in the heavenly places, far above all rule and authority and power and dominion, and above every name that is named, not only in this age but also in the one to come" (Eph 1:19–21). There could be no greater power than this and on this power this personal assurance may rest.

In distinction to this, those passages which picture the return of Christ to the earth as the Messiah King are laden with emphasis upon the fact that He comes with power and great glory. "And then they will see the Son of Man coming in a cloud with power and great glory" (Luke 21:27; Matt 19:28; 24:30; 25:31; Mark 8:38; 13:26; Luke 19:26).

In the final picture at the end of the divine record the culminating event of all past ages is set forth in such majesty as it is possible for language to describe or human minds to comprehend (Rev 19:11–20:15). The Lord of Glory proceeds forth from His wedding, out from heaven, followed by His spotless bride. He comes in "power and great glory." Behold Him as lightning shining from the one part of heaven even unto the other. He has a "rod of iron" in His hand with which to dash the nations "in pieces like a potter's vessel." "His eyes are as a flame of fire" and "from his mouth comes a sharp sword with which to strike down the nations." That lawless one He shall consume with the spirit of His mouth and destroy with the brightness of His coming. He is "revealed from heaven with his mighty angels in flaming fire, inflicting vengeance on those who do not know God and on those who do not obey the gospel of our Lord Jesus" (2 Thess 1:7–8).

> "Behold, the nations are like a drop from a bucket, and are accounted as the dust on the scales; behold, he takes up the coastlands like fine dust. Lebanon would not suffice for fuel, nor are its beasts enough for a burnt offering. All the nations are as nothing before him, they are accounted by him as less than nothing and emptiness.... When he blows on them, and they wither, and the tempest carries them off like stubble" (Isa 40:15–17, 24)

> "God came from Teman, and the Holy One from Mount Paran. *Selah.* His splendor covered the heavens, and the earth was full of his praise. His brightness was like the light; rays flashed from his hand; and there he veiled his power. Before him went pestilence, and plague followed at his heels. He stood and measured the earth; he looked and shook the nations; then the eternal mountains were scattered; the everlasting hills sank low. His were the everlasting ways" (Hab 3:3–6).

> "Our God comes; he does not keep silence; before him is a devouring fire, around him a mighty tempest" (Ps 50:3).

"Who is this who comes from Edom, in crimsoned garments from Bozrah, he who is splendid in his apparel, marching in the greatness of his strength? 'It is I, speaking in righteousness, mighty to save.' Why is your apparel red, and your garments like his who treads in the winepress? 'I have trodden the winepress alone, and from the peoples no one was with me; I trod them in my anger and trampled them in my wrath; their lifeblood spattered on my garments, and stained all my apparel. For the day of vengeance was in my heart, and my year of redemption had come'" (Isa 63:1–4).

Here is the Messenger of the covenant, a Refiner's fire, a purifier of the sons of Levi.

"He will raise a signal for the nations and will assemble the banished of Israel, and gather the dispersed of Judah from the four corners of the earth" (Isa 11:12).

"And he will send out his angels with a loud trumpet call, and they will gather his elect from the four winds, from one end of heaven to the other" (Matt 24:31).

"For he comes, for he comes to judge the earth" (Ps 96:13).

"May desert tribes bow down before him, and his enemies lick the dust! May the kings of Tarshish and of the coastlands render him tribute; may the kings of Sheba and Seba bring gifts! May all kings fall down before him, all nations serve him" (Ps 72:9–11).

"Lift up your heads, O gates! And be lifted up, O ancient doors, that the King of glory may come in. Who is this King of glory? The LORD, strong and mighty, the LORD, mighty in battle" (Ps 24:7–8).

Here is an unfolding of the sufficiency of God in His power to transform the earth and to change the shadow of darkness and sin to the ineffable light of His glory. What He has promised will He not fulfill? All of the lines of hope from the first promise of final victory given in Eden to the present hour are focused upon the return of the King in His power, majesty and strength, and He will compass every issue of the ages and vindicate every purpose of God. It is not a marvel that He should come in renovating judgments to the earth: the marvel must ever be that He, the King of Glory, should bow the heavens and come down to this earth as an unresisting Lamb. The great conquerors of the earth have been mere men who by personality, or favorable conditions, were able to marshal the allegiance of an army of sufficient strength to execute their will; but this One will not be dependent upon a majority and the brute force it represents. His power by which all things were created is sufficient to transform the whole universe, to bind all the forces of darkness and to consummate the hopes of the ages.

Beginning with Revelation 19:11 there is given the final picture of the return of Christ in power and great glory. Preceding this the Patmos Seer has recorded the events of the great tribulation, the appearance and reign of the Beast, the man of lawlessness, and the casting of Satan and his host into the earth. Into the midst of this indescribable anarchy, wickedness and confusion the King appears. And He appears in all His glory. That glory is fourfold.

Ezekiel had seen the celestial beings who are ever before the face of Jehovah and who reflect His glory. Their faces were four: the face of a man, the face of a lion, the face of an ox, and the face of an eagle. There is striking agreement here with the divine manifestation as revealed in the four Gospels. Matthew portrays the Lion King, Mark the Servant Ox, Luke the Man Christ Jesus, and John the Son of God, fittingly symbolized by the eagle. Christ is the sum total of these four revelations. In each manifestation there is a particular glory to be seen: As the Son of

God, He had a glory with the Father before the world was; His eternal glory. As the Son of David, He will have another glory, of which the glory of Solomon was only a feeble type. As the Servant of Jehovah, He has a personal glory; for "it is more blessed to give than to receive," and He was among them as one who served. As the Son of Man He had an acquired glory, a name above every name is given unto Him because of His obedience unto death. It is Luke who unfolds the mysteries of the physical birth, childhood and development of the man Christ Jesus. In this Gospel every coloring is of the Son of Man who "came to seek and to save the lost."

The four names ascribed to Christ in the final description of His return in power and glory again imply His fourfold glory, and His return is in that full glory of the only begotten of the Father. In this description He is first mentioned as "Faithful and True." This is Jehovah's Servant the Ox, the portrait given to Mark. Under this title it is said of Him that "he judges and makes war. His eyes are like a flame of fire, and on his head are many diadems."

A second title ascribed to Him is "The Word of God." The eternal Logos of the Gospel of John. To this title no words seem to be added other than that His saints, His bride, are seen following Him clothed in the spotless white; the "righteousness of God" (2 Cor 5:21; cf. Rev 19:7–8); for they shall see Him as He is and be like Him. The third title ascribed to Him is of a "name written that no one knows but himself." And with this title it is said "He is clothed in a robe dipped in blood" (cf. Isa 63:1–4).

These three characters of the Christ are again seen in Philippians 2:5–11. As the Word of God He was equal with the Father, but deemed that equality no prize to be seized upon. As the Servant of Jehovah, He made Himself of no reputation and took upon Him the form of a servant and was made in the likeness of a man. Under the unrevealed title, "name written that no one knows but himself," He humbled Himself and became obedient unto death, even the death of the cross. In Hebrews 10:5–7, He is seen freely yielding His own body to the will of the Father as a sacrifice, thus bringing into full contrast the insufficiency of the former offerings of bulls and goats: "But a body have you prepared for me; in burnt offerings and sin offerings you have taken no pleasure. Then I said, 'Behold, I have come to do your will, O God, as it is written of me in the scroll of the book.'"

Returning to the passage in Philippians 2:5–11, it may be seen that because of this obedience "to the point of death, even death on a cross," "God has highly exalted him and bestowed on him the name that is above every name, so that at the name of Jesus every knee should bow, in heaven and on earth and under the earth, and every tongue confess that Jesus Christ is Lord, to the glory of God the Father."

"Jesus" then is the name which no man can know. "You shall call his name Jesus, for he will save his people from their sins." Locked up in this name are the fathomless mercies of God. Who can know the meaning of that obedience, or of that cross? Who can understand His atoning sacrificial death? Eternity cannot suffice to unfold His manifold grace. Truly "Jesus" is a name the full meaning of which "no one knows, but himself."

Christ is lastly seen in the final picture of His return under the fourth title of "King of kings and Lord of lords," and gathers into Himself a far greater glory, as David's Son, than has yet been known by all the royal families of the earth.

Thus when He shall come in power and great glory that power will be for the transformation of a sin darkened earth, and in that glory will be combined the ineffable glory of the Servant of Jehovah, the Word of God, the acquired glory of the cross, and the earthly glory of the Son of David, King of kings and Lord of lords.

In such a glory His bride will share. For "When Christ who is your life appears, then you also will appear with him in glory" (Col 3:4). But that outward glory is incomparable with the consolation of the secret chamber where the bride will be at home in the bosom of the Bridegroom. Every tear will be wiped away and with undimmed eye we shall gaze upon His face and go out no more forever.

14

"Your Kingdom Come"

The return of Christ, as anticipated in Scripture, is the consummation of all the great purposes of God. It is impossible to seriously trace the mighty movements developed in Scripture without finding that their ultimate issues and realization are dependent upon one of the great events connected with the second coming of Christ. It cannot therefore be expected that a thorough knowledge of the Bible, or a deep interest in its teachings, will be gained apart from the key to Scriptures which His coming forms. Certain historical and doctrinal passages may become familiar, and a self-satisfied mind, which insulates itself from all added light, may result; but this is far removed from the vision which is gained by a life study of the whole text of Scripture.

Real study of the Bible is a habit which is not acquired through educational courses, nor is it apt to be gained later on when the cares of a mature life and the strategy of Satan in keeping these to the fore hinder the gaining of such a blessed, power-giving, sanctifying habit in the child of God. We wrestle against Satan in the higher sphere of heavenly association and realities rather than in the lower sphere of flesh and blood (Eph 6:10–12), and few are awake to claim their deliverance from his withering touch in the most vital issues of their new life and being. A multitude of ministers must confess that they do not actually and habitually study the Bible for themselves, though they may occasionally read it for others. Weak indeed it is for such an one to hastily denounce the only interpretation that will fairly account for the whole body of Truth and which has been the unanimous conclusion of the most eminent Bible expositors throughout the age (knowledge of the-

ology which may depend upon certain proof texts is incomparable with
the fuller knowledge of the Scriptures required for exposition); nor is
it safe under present conditions, in the face of personal ignorance, to
blindly hide behind the opinion of a supposed, or actual majority. All
true ministry and service must have a goal, or objective as an incentive in
view. Naturally this should be the determination to realize the present
purpose of God. The servant, at best, will be as his Lord and thus be
intelligently aiming at the immediate divine objective, knowing that the
ultimate blessings can be secured by no other program.

There is to be a kingdom of righteousness in the earth: it does not
follow, however, that its establishment is the present purpose of God, or
that the saved ones of this age are to form its subjects. Such a conclusion
might be gained from human guesses, or superficial reading, but could
hardly be the result of careful study of "present truth" as presented in the
New Testament. There will be no establishment of an earthly kingdom
apart from the coming and presence of the King and that event, in turn,
must await the accomplishment of all divine purposes in this mystery
age. To be intelligently adjusted to the present divine undertakings is to
be committed to a very special form of service and to be working toward
a very different goal than the bringing in of a kingdom by undertaking
worldwide conversion. It is a matter of obedience to the more simple
direction to evangelize all nations, which is not to be done once for all
as an objective, but must be done anew with each succeeding generation
until the real objective is accomplished—the out-calling of the church.
Apart from the question of divine command, the earthly blessings will
be conceded to be nearer when depending on His imminent return
than when resting upon any approach to worldwide conversion that has
yet been displayed. Is not the testimony of nineteen centuries sufficient
witness to the divine purpose in this age apart from revelation? If we
believe that God is able to realize His own will and purpose at a given
time, we must conclude that worldwide conversion has not been His
present age purpose. It is needless to add that He is suffering no such
defeat, but is faithfully following the exact plan He has disclosed in His
Word. It is for every child of God to know the exact plan He has disclosed
and to be wholly subject to it, else his ignorant service may but play into

the hands of the enemy of God and add to the final bonfire of wood, hay and stubble.

In the Scriptures the return of Christ is presented as a full development of the purpose of God.

First, it accomplishes the cessation of much of the present form of evil. A theory that evil will grow less and less until it vanishes from the earth is not a doctrine of the Scriptures. There sin is faithfully traced from its beginning in the fall of Satan, and is seen to run its course and to be suddenly terminated in the hour of its fullest manifestation; and all this is in the permissive will and restraining power of God. The following Scriptures show that the return of Christ will terminate the sin and confusion of the earth: 2 Thessalonians 2:7–10; Daniel 2:44; 7:13, 14; Malachi 4:1; Jude 1:14, 15; Matthew 24:15–30; Revelation 11:7–13:18; 19:11–20:3.

Second, as certainly as the saved ones of this dispensation have all their hope and blessing in the heavenly glory so certainly it all awaits His coming to claim His own. Even those who have fallen asleep in Jesus await their immortal bodies and that blessed marriage to Him. All saints await His coming to receive His bride (John 14:1–3). Their rewards will then be bestowed (2 Tim 4:8; 2 Cor 5 :10). Their marriage bliss awaits His call (Rev 19:7–8). So, also, the appointments to authority as co-reigners with Him (Rev 2:6, 27; 20:6). How can the church, if she be true to the spiritual vision, do otherwise than to pray, "Amen, even so, come Lord Jesus"?

Third, the final Gentile blessings await His return, as well as their judgment as nations. Two Gentile purposes are now revealed: first, He is visiting the Gentiles to call out a bride; and second, there will be universal Gentile blessing when the kingdom is finally manifested in the earth (Acts 15:14–18; Rom 15:8–12; Mal 1:11; Jer 16:19; Isa 11:10).

Fourth, creation must groan and travail until His return:

> "For the creation waits with eager longing for the revealing of the sons of God" (Rom 8:19).

But when will they be manifested?

"When Christ who is your life appears, then you also will
appear with him in glory" (Col 3:4).

"For the creation was subjected to futility, not willingly, but because of
him who subjected it, in hope that the creation itself will be set free from
its bondage to corruption and obtain the freedom of the glory of the
children of God. For we know that the whole creation has been groaning
together in the pains of childbirth until now. And not only the creation,
but we ourselves, who have the firstfruits of the Spirit, groan inwardly
as we wait eagerly for adoption as sons, the redemption of our bodies"
(Rom 8:20–23).

This, too, is a well-defined time, "But our citizenship is in heaven, and
from it we await a Savior, the Lord Jesus Christ, who will transform our
lowly body to be like his glorious body" (Phil 3:20–21). All creation,
then, awaits the deliverance and blessing that will be wrought by His
return.

Fifth, His return in glory ushers in the earthly kingdom and ends
the long night of Israel's affliction. Their Messiah truly cometh, but
in His own time. From the following passages, which might be greatly
multiplied, it may be concluded that there is no divine expectation of the
long-awaited earthly kingdom apart from the return of the King as He
comes in power and great glory: Deuteronomy 30:3; Psalm 1:1–6; Daniel
2:44, 45; 7:13, 14; Zechariah 2:10–12; 14:4–8; Malachi 4:1–4; Matthew
24:30, 31, 34; Romans 11:25–27; Revelation 12:9, 10; 19:11–20:6.

Three accounts are given in the Scriptures of the transfiguration, and
each is preceded by the significant words: "There are some standing
here who will not taste death until they see the Son of Man coming in
his kingdom." The meaning of the transfiguration is given by Peter, an
"eyewitness":

"For we did not follow cleverly devised myths when we
made known to you the power and coming of our Lord

Jesus Christ, but we were eyewitnesses of his majesty. For
when he received honor and glory from God the Father,
and the voice was borne to him by the Majestic Glory,
'This is my beloved Son, with whom I am well pleased,'
we ourselves heard this very voice borne from heaven, for
we were with him on the holy mountain" (2 Pet 1:16–18).

Here Peter affirms by the Spirit that the scene on the holy mountain
was a revelation of the "power and coming of the Lord Jesus Christ." The
essential elements of the future earthly kingdom were all represented in
this scene. Christ appears in His heavenly glory; two were with Him,
sharing in the glory. One had gone to be with the Lord by death, and one
by translation; but both were equally glorified together with the Lord.
Upon the earth were representatives of the chosen nation. These were
not in the transfiguration glory, but were in such blessing that one could
say, "It is good that we are here." So shall it be in the final manifestation
of the Messianic kingdom in the earth. The church will be with Him and
share His glory and reign. The nation, and through them all nations, will
live in His millennial blessing and reign. There were some standing there
who did not taste death until they saw the Son of Man coming in His
kingdom.

To fully outline the character and blessedness of that coming age
would require the quotation of a great portion of the messages of the
prophets in which language seems to fail them to fully paint the glory of
the transformed earth. A selection of passages, indicating the character of
the Messianic kingdom, has been given in Chapter 3. By these Scriptures
this kingdom is seen to be:

1. Theocratic. The King will be Immanuel and by human birth
   a rightful heir to David's throne. Himself born of a virgin in
   Bethlehem of Judea.

2. Immanuel's kingdom will be heavenly in character in that the
   God of heaven will rule in the earth. His will to be done in earth
   as it is done in heaven.

3. Immanuel's kingdom will be in the earth, rather than in heaven, and centered at Jerusalem. His blessed reign will be over re-gathered and converted Israel and extend through them to the nations.

4. Immanuel's kingdom will be realized only by virtue of the pow-er and presence of the returning King.

5. Immanuel's kingdom, though material and political, will be spiritual in that its subjects will walk on the earth in the undimmed light of God. The animal kingdom will be subdued:

"The wolf shall dwell with the lamb, and the leopard shall lie down with the young goat, and the calf and the lion and the fattened calf together; and a little child shall lead them. The cow and the bear shall graze; their young shall lie down together; and the lion shall eat straw like the ox. The nursing child shall play over the hole of the cobra, and the weaned child shall put his hand on the adder's den. They shall not hurt or destroy in all my holy mountain; for the earth shall be full of the knowledge of the LORD as the waters cover the sea" (Isa 11:6–9).

So, also, the physical creation shall be changed:

"For you shall go out in joy and be led forth in peace; the mountains and the hills before you shall break forth into singing, and all the trees of the field shall clap their hands. Instead of the thorn shall come up the cypress; instead of the brier shall come up the myrtle; and it shall make a name for the LORD, an everlasting sign that shall not be cut off" (Isa 55:12–13).

"When the poor and needy seek water, and there is none, and their tongue is parched with thirst, I the LORD will answer them; I the God of Israel will not forsake them. I will open rivers on the bare heights, and fountains in the midst of the valleys. I will make the wilderness a pool of water, and the dry land springs of water. I will put in the wilderness the cedar, the acacia, the myrtle, and the olive. I will set in the desert the cypress, the plane and the pine together, that they may see and know, may consider and understand together, that the hand of the LORD has done this, the Holy One of Israel has created it" (Isa 41:17–20).

"For the earth will be filled with the knowledge of the glory of the LORD as the waters cover the sea" (Hab 2:14).

"Blessed are the meek, for they shall inherit the earth" (Matt 5:5).

"He shall judge between many peoples, and shall decide disputes for strong nations far away; and they shall beat their swords into plowshares, and their spears into pruning hooks; nation shall not lift up sword against nation, neither shall they learn war anymore" (Mic 4:3).

"Then the eyes of the blind shall be opened, and the ears of the deaf unstopped; then shall the lame man leap like a deer, and the tongue of the mute sing for joy. For waters break forth in the wilderness, and streams in the desert" (Isa 35:5–6).

"For this is the covenant that I will make with the house of Israel after those days, declares the LORD: I will put my law within them, and I will write it on their hearts.

And I will be their God, and they shall be my people. And no longer shall each one teach his neighbor and each his brother, saying, 'Know the LORD,' for they shall all know me, from the least of them to the greatest, declares the LORD. For I will forgive their iniquity, and I will remember their sin no more" (Jer 31:33–34).

"For to us a child is born, to us a son is given; and the government shall be upon his shoulder, and his name shall be called Wonderful Counselor, Mighty God, Everlasting Father, Prince of Peace. Of the increase of his government and of peace there will be no end, on the throne of David and over his kingdom, to establish it and to uphold it with justice and with righteousness from this time forth and forevermore. The zeal of the LORD of hosts will do this" (Isa 9:6–7).

"May he have dominion from sea to sea, and from the River to the ends of the earth! May desert tribes bow down before him, and his enemies lick the dust! May the kings of Tarshish and of the coastlands render him tribute; may the kings of Sheba and Seba bring gifts! May all kings fall down before him, all nations serve him! ... May his name endure forever, his fame continue as long as the sun! May people be blessed in him, all nations call him blessed! Blessed be the LORD, the God of Israel, who alone does wondrous things. Blessed be his glorious name forever; may the whole earth be filled with his glory! Amen and Amen" (Ps 72:8–11, 17–19).

Such is Immanuel's kingdom in the earth. Such is the covenant of peace with Israel forever.

At the close of this millennium of peace and righteousness there is the dark picture of the final testing of all willing separation from God in the loosing of Satan for a "little while" and the war that follows. The Great White Throne is set; its judgment is past; and lo, the new heavens and new earth wherein dwells righteousness. The revolt of earth and the powers of darkness against the sovereignty of God is forever past.

> "Then comes the end, when he delivers the kingdom to God the Father after destroying every rule and every authority and power. For he must reign until he has put all his enemies under his feet" (1 Cor 15:24–25).

> "Your kingdom come, your will be done, on earth as it is in heaven" (Matt 6:10).

www.ingramcontent.com/pod-product-compliance
Lightning Source LLC
Chambersburg PA
CBHW071522120626
46550CB00006B/2317